/

M

SEP 0 1 1904

TARAWA

TARAWA

Charles T. Gregg

𝕾𝖉

STEIN AND DAY/*Publishers*/New York

ACKNOWLEDGMENTS

As in my two previous books I have benefited greatly from critical readings of this manuscript by both personal friends and by colleagues with special knowledge that they were able to bring to bear on the subject of this book.

Dr. Ernest C. Anderson, a scholar of immense breadth of learning, Lt. Col. John G. Celli, (USMC, ret.), and William Johnson (formerly a World War II Scout-Sniper with the 3rd Marine Division in the Pacific), each read the entire manuscript and made important suggestions.

Robert H. Boulton and John R. Williams, both formerly signalmen aboard the antiaircraft cruiser *Oakland* and the destroyer *Sigsbee*, respectively, generously shared with me their experiences during the Gilbert Islands campaign.

Mr. Patrick McKiernan of The Morgan School, Clinton, Connecticut, kindly made available to me his notes from an interview he conducted with Admiral Harry Hill in September 1960.

Finally, my wife continued to be supportive of my penchant for writing books, although skeptical of my promise never to write another.

Quotations from Robert Sherrod's *Tarawa: The Story of a Battle* are reprinted with the permission of the author.

The quotation from E. J. Wilson's *Betio Beachhead* reprinted by permission of the publisher, G. P. Putnam's Sons.

The quotation from Jeter A. Isely's and Philip A. Crowl's *The U.S. Marines and Amphibious War: Its Theory, and Its Practice in the Pacific*, Copyright 1951, © renewed 1979, reprinted by permission of the publisher, Princeton University Press.

The quotation from Edwin Hoyt's *How They Won the War in the Pacific: Nimitz and His Admirals*, reprinted by permission of the publisher, Weybright and Talley.

The quotation from Samuel E. Morison's *History of U.S. Naval Operations in World War Two* reprinted by permission of the publisher, Little, Brown and Company.

All photos and paintings are printed courtesy of the U.S. Department of Defense.

The map of the Pacific theater is from Mark Arnold-Forster's *The World at War* and is reprinted courtesy of Stein and Day/*Publishers*.

Library of Congress Cataloging in Publication Data

Gregg, Charles T.
    Tarawa.

    Bibliography: p.
    Includes index.
    1. Tarawa, Battle of, 1943.   I. Title.
D767.917.G73   1983   940.54′26   83-42972
ISBN 0-8128-2906-9

To the memory of General David Monroe Shoup, 1907-1983

Contents

Illustrations

(Illustrations on pages 103 through 118)

Maps

Foreword

Many books have been written about the battle for Tarawa Atoll. These have generally concentrated on the struggle of the marines to overcome the stout and well-planned Japanese resistance. There are, however, other dimensions to the battle. In Operation Galvanic, of which the winning of Tarawa Atoll was the major part, airmen and sailors also died, some of them without ever seeing the island. Moreover, Tarawa had a substantial role in the development of tactics and strategy for the Pacific war, and its significance can best be understood in the context of how that war came to be and what major military actions preceded it in the Pacific.

The aim of this book is to place the battle for Tarawa Atoll—an event now forty years in the past as this book comes into being—into its proper historical perspective while still telling the story of courage, ingenuity, and discipline that led to victory there as well as elsewhere in the Pacific.

TARAWA

1

NO TIME FOR
MAGGIE'S DRAWERS

From the very beginning the decision of the Joint Chiefs to seize
Tarawa was a mistake and from their initial mistake grew the
terrible drama of errors, errors of omission rather than commission, resulting in these needless casualties.

General Holland M. Smith, U.S. Marine Corps (Ret.), 1949.

It was no place for an elderly lady. Still the aged battleship USS *Maryland* (whose keel had been laid in 1916) was steaming northward through
the hot tropic night as flagship of Task Force 53 (TF 53), the Southern
Attack Force.

Less than two years before, the ship had been left torn and burning in
Battleship Row alongside Pearl Harbor's Ford Island as the exultant pilots
of the Japanese carrier planes did their final victory rolls and turned back
toward their home fleet. *Maryland* had not sunk only because the battleship *Oklahoma*, moored to seaward of her, had taken the brunt of the
attack, three torpedoes in sixty seconds, two more a moment later. *Oklahoma* capsized and sank. Aft of *Maryland*, the burning battleships *West
Virginia* and *Arizona* poured great columns of oily smoke into the darken-
ing sky.

Now, in November 1943, *Maryland*, repaired and refitted, had arrived in
the South Pacific for her reentry into the war as a fighting ship despite the
fact that Radio Tokyo had reported her sunk on five separate occasions
after Pearl Harbor.

From aboard *Maryland*, Rear Adm. Harry W. Hill commanded TF 53. Harry Hill, fifty-three years old, was as lean and quick moving as when he had been both bow oar on the Naval Academy rowing team and a champion high hurdler. His hair was just beginning to gray above his blue eyes, and he was constantly breaking into a merry smile. He had served on *Maryland* before, as gunnery officer from 1928 to 1931, now he commanded the armada fanning out around the flagship.

At eight bells (midnight) Saturday, November 20, 1943, Admiral Hill ordered a forty-five degree right turn, and thirty-eight helmsmen briskly turned their wheels until their ships' compass needles steadied on 045 degrees, and the thirty-eight ships of the Southern Attack Force took up a new course.

Forty-five minutes later, a Marine bugler saluted the Officer Of the Deck on *Maryland*'s bridge and asked the traditional question, "Reveille on time, sir?" Tension was building on the bridge and the OOD's answer was curt, "On time." After a few practice notes, the bugler stepped to the ship's intercom and the raucous notes of reveille rang through the ship. The bugler was followed by the boatswain's mate (called "Boats" in Navy slang) whose silver whistle and strident voice repeated the bugler's message, "Reveille, reveille. All hands, reveille. Up all bunks."

"Boats" and the bugler grinned at each other as they saw that their exhortations had seemingly roused a sluggard, gibbous moon from some distant sea, and it, too, rose sleepily to cast a wan light across the southern ocean.

The vessels rushed on in total darkness that they might stealthily approach their enemy. Yet, as the steel bows cleaved the waters, billions of miniscule sea creatures ignited their tiny lanterns in terror, and great phosphorescent streaks curved down the flanks of every ship and coalesced into a brightly glowing wake astern. To an alert pilot of a marauding "Betty" (the formidable Mitsubishi Zero-1 medium bomber) the shining wakes were like arrows pointing to targets. Fortunately, no Bettys nor other Japanese reconnaissance aircraft appeared, and the convoy's speed, limited to under fourteen knots by the slow transports, showed a minimal wake compared with that churned up by warships at full speed.

The morning of the previous day a four-engined Japanese reconnaissance plane (called a "Mavis" by American forces) had been spotted by radar sixty miles west of Task Force 53. The plane was quickly shot down by the combat air patrol of the escort carrier *Suwannee*. But no one knew whether the crew of the Mavis had advised Japanese headquarters of the powerful forces sailing against it.

The destroyers of the escort screen had made a submarine contact the previous night. They had attacked with depth charges, and the sonar contact had disappeared. About this time the big Japanese submarine *I-25* disappeared from the rolls of the Mikado's fighting ships, but it is uncertain whether or not it was the attack of TF 53's destroyers that finished her.

Reveille came a little later aboard the twelve attack transports than aboard the flagship. For many of the men who had spent the night marinating in their own sweat as they alternately stared at the bottom of the bunk above them or at the gray walls of the sleeping compartments faintly illuminated by battle lanterns, reveille was a welcome relief. Action would replace waiting. After two weeks at sea they were ready.

The marines, sailors, and coastguardsmen were naturally apprehensive. Most would taste fear, many terror, before the fat moon rose again.

Over half of the marines were veterans of the invasion of Guadalcanal. Although the Second Marine Division, whose men now dressed for the roles they would play in the looming drama, had not made the initial landing on Guadalcanal, they had heard about it from their comrades of the First Division. The only casualty had been a marine who cut himself while opening a coconut. Would it be like that on Tarawa?

Opinions were divided. Some marines thought it would be another Kiska. When the Army charged ashore through the icy Alaskan fog to take that remote island, in late July 1943, they found that the Japanese defenders had slipped away, unnoticed in the murky darkness.

A surgeon aboard the transport *Zeilin* predicted, "There won't be a damned Jap on Tarawa."

Betio Island (pronounced Bayshio), the only strategically important portion of Tarawa Atoll, had been pounded for days by the four-engined Liberators (B-24s) of the Army's Seventh Air Force and by the dive-bombers, torpedo planes, and fighters of the U.S. Navy. Due to the great distances involved, land-based aircraft made only 259 sorties against the Gilberts (of which Tarawa Atoll was a part) and the Marshalls during November 1943, compared with 2,284 sorties on the same targets by carrier-based aircraft. The total number of bombs dropped by the latter was nearly fourfold higher, too, although little significant damage was done by either group. Every day for a week before the Betio landing, Liberators hit every surrounding airfield they could reach to eliminate interference with the invasion and retard staging of Japanese planes into the area.

There also steamed with the convoy through the tepid seas two other venerable battleships, *Tennessee* and *Colorado*, both in service for twenty years or more, the ten-year-old cruisers *Portland* and *Indianapolis*, the new light cruisers *Santa Fe*, *Birmingham*, and *Mobile*, along with twenty-one destroyers and five escort carriers. The latter carried, in all, 134 planes that would batter Betio while the naval vessels pounded it with their big guns from as close to the atoll as they could get.

Naval bombardment could drive a man mad. The marines knew it, especially those who had been on Guadalcanal on the nights of August 19-20 and on the still more nightmarish October 14, 1942, when the battleships *Haruna* and *Kongo* with their sixteen big guns and far more numerous small ones had poured shells, from five to fourteen inches in diameter, onto the island as fast as the gunners could reload them. They had begun firing incendiary shells and then switched to armor-piercing munitions. The October shelling, which had begun at 0100, lasted for the longest ninety-seven minutes in anyone's memory and left the island in shambles. Nearly 1,000 rounds of fourteen-inch shells had been hurled onto the island and a smaller force repeated the performance the following night. There had once been skeptics. Major Gen. Archer A. Vandergrift, the Marine commander on Guadalcanal, tells of the doctor and chaplain who were discussing combat fatigue in his command post one night early in the campaign. The doctor said, "Look at us. We're all much older and we're not touched by it." The chaplain naturally averred that faith was the answer. Later, because of their psychological states after a prolonged shelling, although neither was injured, both the doctor and the chaplain had to be evacuated. The marines almost felt sorry for the Japanese on Betio. If there were any.

The boast of Rear Adm. Howard F. Kingman (commanding the Gunfire Support Group of three battleships, three light and two heavy cruisers, and nine destroyers) had circulated throughout TF 53. In a briefing of division officers at Efate, he had said, "It is not our intention to wreck the island. We do not intend to destroy it. Gentlemen, we will obliterate it!" A group of marines agreed that they would take Betio in eight hours. It was, after all, less than half a square mile in area, or only slightly more than one-third the size of New York's Central Park. The supply officers seemed to concur. Aboard one of the attack transports were 1,600 half-pints of ice cream to be brought ashore when the battle was over—at the end of the first day!

Not everyone was so optimistic. Major Gen. Julian Smith guessed, reluctantly, that about one-third of the Japanese defenders would be killed by the bombardment, and Col. David Shoup (who would command all forces ashore on Betio) guessed about twenty percent. Col. Merritt A. "Red Mike" Edson, chief of staff of the Second Marine Division, was a tall, husky, slightly stoop-shouldered, blond marine who had fought his country's battles for nearly twenty years, from the jungles of Nicaragua to the green hell of Guadalcanal. On the 'Canal he had won a Congressional Medal of Honor. As Red Mike put it, "We cannot count on heavy naval and air bombardment to kill all the Japs on Tarawa, or even a large proportion of them. Neither can we count on taking Tarawa, small as it is, in a few hours." Red Mike smiled, but only with his mouth. His pale blue eyes gleamed, in war correspondent R. W. Johnston's phrase, "with the impersonal menace of pistol muzzles."

A grizzled Marine sergeant put it differently. "We know the Navy is going to hit that damned island with everything there is. But something in the back of my mind tells me there's going to be a lot of shooting Japs left when we start going ashore."

Clearly someone was going to be wrong.

On the last night before the landing, Marine Major Gen. Julian C. Smith, commanding the Second Marine Division, sent a message to his men from the flagship. "We are the first American troops to attack a defended atoll. What we do here will set a standard for all future operations in the Central Pacific area." After that bit of prophecy it concluded, "I know you are well trained and fit for the tasks assigned to you. You will quickly overrun the Japanese forces; you will decisively defeat and destroy the treacherous enemies of our country; your success will add new laurels to the glories of our Corps. Good luck and God bless you all."

Breakfast on the transports was steak, scrambled eggs, and fried potatoes. It was served beginning at the very unfashionable hour of 2200 (10:00 p.m.). There was plenty of strong black coffee, and there was a pervasive air of fear and excitement that can take the place of food. Some of the men would eat little or nothing for twenty-four hours and never notice it. It would be just as well. As one Navy surgeon remarked as he watched the young men wolfing down their breakfasts, "Jesus, that'll make a nice lot of guts to sew up—full of steak." There would be many abdominal wounds. And large numbers of the wounded would bleed to death, drown, or be operated on by the surgical teeth of sharks before they could get medical attention. Days later, a Navy pilot would report large numbers of bodies floating out to sea from Tarawa. He thought they were Japanese; many were U.S. Marines.

To reduce wound infection (in this pre-antibiotic era), the marines had been ordered to put on clean uniforms that morning. But in the oppressive tropical heat and humidity the clean uniforms were soggy with sweat before the men had even finished tying their "boondockers" (combat boots).

Beginning at 0130 (1:30 a.m.), the heart-stopping klaxons began to sound General Quarters; throughout the Southern Attack Force men went to their battle stations. At five minutes after two, Rear Admiral Hill gave the order for a second forty-five degree turn to starboard, and Task Force 53 swung ponderously to ninety degrees (due east). Forty-five minutes later the sinister outline of the island of Betio, code-named Helen, was sighted from the bridge of *Maryland*. The island lay low in the water, the highest point of land was barely ten feet above sea level, and silhouetted against the half-grown moon. By 0320 the transports were some six miles west of Betio, and the ships of the task force hove to in the predawn darkness.

There was considerable tension on the thirty-eight ships' bridges. Lieutenant Charles Wilkes, USN had visited the Gilberts in 1841. He had reported that the women were the prettiest in the South Seas, and he charted the area. But Wilkes's charts, as used by the invasion force more than a century later, bore such notations as: "Use these charts with caution," or "This chart should be used with circumspection—the surveys are incomplete." As Rear Adm. A. Stanton Merrill had put it in a similar situation: "The possibility of viewing the sunrise from the sloping deck of a ship stranded on an uncharted shoal is a thought not pleasant to contemplate, especially if said shoal is under the guns of the enemy's coast-defense batteries."

Admiral Hill and his colleagues also used the latest British Admiralty charts of Tarawa Atoll, but these had Betio Island wrongly oriented; the island's axis was given as 139 degrees when it was really 128 degrees. Fortunately, the submarine *Nautilus* had discovered this error in a reconnaissance and reported it to the task force.

Now landing craft were secured to davits, and the shrilling of bosun's pipes and the whining of motors intermingled in the tropic night as the small craft were hoisted from the decks and holds of transports, swung over the sides, and lowered into the calm southern ocean, while Marine sergeants called roll and gave last minute instructions to ensure accurate shooting. On the Marine boot camp firing ranges a bright red flag, known in the Corps as "Maggie's drawers," was hoisted when a boot completely missed the target. Humiliating as that was, the punishment for bad shooting on Betio might be much more serious.

The sergeants giving final words of wisdom to their men reminded them not to shout each other's names. A Japanese sniper would shout the same name a few minutes later and shoot the marine who stuck up his head to answer. The sergeants chose to ignore the fact that some of the marines were shaking with malarial chills and fever, a consequence of their time on Guadalcanal, but had nonetheless lined up in uniform with their "782 gear" to go ashore and fight at the side of their buddies.*

There were 17,000 men in the Second Marine Division as the ships sailed from the harbor of Wellington, New Zealand. Of that number only sixteen had gone AWOL before sailing, and only four on the last day. Usually a division could expect to lose about one percent when it sailed into combat, so a little more than 150 AWOLs would have been expected.

Then it was discovered that the transports were south of their assigned positions. All operations stopped while they moved north. This was the first delay in the assault on Betio.

Ships' chaplains gave general absolution to the Catholics, and one coastguardsman who was to go ashore as part of a Navy beach party was annoyed with himself when he found he could only remember the first two sentences of the Lord's Prayer.

Landing nets were lowered over the sides of the twelve transports, and the marines in full combat regalia put their right legs over the rails and climbed down the ropes into the landing craft below. Most of the men wore

---

*The marine's combat equipment was called "782 gear" for the number of the receipt they signed to get it. Although the receipt form and number have changed several times the name remains.

green cloth helmet covers and green jungle dungarees. Some unfortunates wore an experimental reversible uniform mottled green on one side, mottled brown on the other. The reversible uniform proved unbearably hot and was never used again. Each man carried his weapons and enough ammunition (called a unit of fire) for one day's combat. He also had two canteens of water, a shaving kit, a toothbrush, a spoon, and three packages of K rations. The average pack weight was an incredible eighty-four pounds (twenty more than the Japanese carried). Some men carried even more, twenty-pound BARs (Browning Automatic Rifles), forty-five-pound 81-mm mortar base plates, forty-seven-pound mortar bipods, thirty-six-pound light machine guns, forty-one-pound heavy machine guns, or heavy machine-gun tripods that weighed more than fifty-three pounds. Each marine wore a web belt with ammunition pouches. Most were filled with ammunition, but some were used for packages of cigarettes that fit perfectly in the ammunition pouches.

For each marine the attack cargo ships in the task force carried an additional 1,322 pounds of supplies. The three attack transports (*Thuban, Bellatrix,* and *Virgo*) carried a total of 3,000 five-gallon cans of water; 28,200 gallons of high-octane gasoline for the amtracs that would take the first assault waves ashore; five units of fire for all heavy weapons except medium tanks, which had only four; thirty days worth of general supplies; and about 3,000 pounds of chemical-warfare supplies (which were never used). In all, 6,000 vehicles and 117,000 tons of supplies were delivered to the Gilberts for Operation Galvanic.

All of this had come from Pearl Harbor 2,100 miles away. In 1904, a naval officer, A. C. Cunningham, had suggested the concept of a mobile base that would move with the fleet. This concept was employed for the first time in Operation Galvanic. A fleet of support vessels, including nine huge barges (some formerly Mississippi River sugar barges), carrying a thirty-day supply of food and medicine for 20,000 men as well as ammunition, fuel, and spare parts, assembled in Funafuti Lagoon. From this base the barges, accompanied by destroyer escorts, made almost daily trips to the Gilberts. Fuel was also provided by a fleet of thirteen fleet oilers that accompanied the invasion forces; each carried 80,000 barrels of fuel oil (one day's estimated consumption for the Galvanic strike force), 18,000 barrels of aviation gasoline, and nearly 6,800 barrels of diesel fuel. These oilers shuttled between the fleet and groups of other fleet oilers stationed in the area. The latter similarly shuttled between Pearl Harbor and commercial tankers that had been positioned around the South Pacific.

About one large ship was required to transport every 1,100 men. For Operation Galvanic the Navy simply didn't have enough ships to do the job and finally chartered fifteen merchant ships to help out.

Food was not shipped directly from the United States because it was considered more efficient to use large ships to go from the United States to

Pearl Harbor and smaller ships from Pearl westward. Moreover, it was questionable whether Liberty ships could enter the lagoons in the Gilberts, and it was desirable to keep the merchant marine out of the combat zone. In addition, the U.S. Navy had to provision some 30,000 Gilbert Islanders for a month and provide continuous supplies to the garrisons occupying the Gilberts.

When the Second Marine Division landed on Guadalcanal they still carried the Springfield rifle first issued in 1903 and only slightly changed since then. The bolt-action Springfield fired single shots from a five-round clip. When the Army had landed on that island the soldiers had the new Garand M-1. By the time the marines left Guadalcanal about one-fourth of them also carried M-1s. Some had even been obtained legally. The M-1 was semiautomatic. An eight-round clip could be fired as fast as the trigger could be squeezed. That was a real advantage in the thick jungle of Guadalcanal. The M-1, compared with the rugged and reliable Springfield, was inaccurate and temperamental. It malfunctioned constantly, especially under the jungle conditions of mud, rain, and high humidity. The gas-operated semiautomatic mechanism failed during prolonged use, and awkward manual operation had to be used instead; its barrel warped when heated by constant firing so it became even more inaccurate than when it was cold. For precision shooting, Marine snipers still carried the '03 Springfield.

The men awaiting their turn to climb over the sides of the transports joked about sarong-clad beauties waiting to greet them on the beach. They repeated the story of one marine who, after going ashore in a practice landing on a remote New Zealand beach, had gone to the ship's sick bay for the regulation prophylactic treatment to prevent venereal disease after intercourse. This enterprising marine was the only one of the landing party to find complaisant female companionship ashore. He was much envied.

The joking and sea stories stopped when it came time to climb down the landing nets. It was a tricky business. The marines had to remember to hold on to only the vertical strands of line or risk getting their fingers stepped on by the man above. If a man fell between the bobbing transport and the even more wildly gyrating landing craft, he risked being crushed between the two steel hulls. It was even worse for the men whose landing craft were alongside the bows or the stern of the ship. There the cargo nets hung free of the ship's side, and with the weight of their packs and weapons, the marines tended to turn upside down in midair. Everyone had to time his leap into the landing craft for the peak of the small boat's upward surge (or the instant after). Otherwise the marine could land in a heap on the steel deck with one or both ankles sprained or broken.

Other marines prayed, talked quietly, or simply watched the stars that glinted down impersonally on the frantic human activity below. It was a beautiful night. The breeze was brisk but warm. The sea was gentle. The stars and moon dodging between scattered clouds gave a diffuse light that created an air of tranquil beauty over Tarawa Atoll to the south—an atoll soon to be writhing in flames and drenched with blood.

When the landing craft were filled they circled endlessly astern of the transports (reminding one observer of a herd of circus elephants waddling trunk to tail) as they waited for the signal to form into waves that would hit the beach on Betio. The men of the first three waves were in amphibious tractors officially known as LVTs (for Landing Vehicle, Tracked), but universally called amtracs. They seemed to do everything but fly. Amtracs were self-propelled through the water, and could climb over coral reefs and run up on beaches to discharge their cargos of fifteen to twenty marines at any suitable place. The first amtracs used in North Africa and Guadalcanal had stalled in the water and either threw their tracks or wore them down quickly when on shore. But the Marine Corps had faith in the little vessels and had continued to improve them. In 1943, the amtracs cost about $35,000 each, an enormous sum at a time when a good living wage in the United States was $2,000 a year or less.

Marvelous as the amtracs were they were far from perfect. They had a prodigious appetite for high-octane gasoline requiring that the three attack cargo ships carry 224 gallons of fuel for each LVT. These vehicles became unmanageable in even a mildly turbulent sea and they were difficult to maneuver under any circumstances. They had very little freeboard; even small waves washed over their low sides and soaked the waiting men. For this same reason they quickly filled and sank when stalled at sea. The amtracs were slow, and they had no ramp that could be dropped to let the men out. The marines had to climb over the sides, exposing themselves to enemy fire, and then drop to the beach or into the surf. Moreover, at least half the amtracs used in the first three assault waves were the older models brought from Guadalcanal; they were lightly armed and lightly armored, and their service lifetime was spectacularly short. The fifty new LVT-2s had 250-hp engines in place of the 146-hp engine used in the older machines, and they were better armored. They were also a bit faster in the water and much faster on land. In any case, without the amtracs there would have been no effective landing on Betio. Their use as assault vessels, carried out for the first time on Betio, was one of the great tactical innovations of the Pacific war.

One of the amtracs took aboard a thirty-four-man special Scout-Sniper Platoon commanded by twenty-nine-year-old First Lt. William D. Hawkins of El Paso, Texas. On Guadalcanal Lieutenant Hawkins and a few men had vanished for three days behind the Japanese lines. They built no fires and buried the empty cans that had contained their cold rations. When they returned from patrol they had Japanese maps, battle plans, and other valuable papers. Most of the original owners of the documents lay dead in the jungle, their throats having been quietly cut to avoid raising an alarm. For this action Lieutenant Hawkins won a commendation. He was to earn a far greater accolade on Tarawa Atoll.

The Scout-Snipers were a unique group. One marine who went through the six-week training program in jungle warfare on American Samoa, followed by the equally long special scout-sniper training, subsequently took part in three harrowing campaigns, Bougainville (beginning three weeks before the Tarawa landing), Guam, and Iwo Jima. To this day he says that the worst experience he ever went through was the training program on Samoa. Everything after that ordeal was relatively easy.

The marines scheduled to land on Betio after the first three waves were ashore were in Higgins boats, officially called LCVPs (Landing Craft, Vehicles and Personnel). These propeller-driven craft held more men than the amtracs. But their most important characteristic in regard to the Betio Island landing was that to avoid running aground they needed nearly four feet of water. The job of the skippers (coxswains) of the Higgins boats was to get the vessel as close to the beach as possible, drop its front ramp, quickly debark troops, then return to the transports for more men or supplies.

So far, the problems were being overcome. The fleet was in position, or nearly so. Unmarked currents had displaced the ships further south than they were intended to be, and within range of the Japanese guns, so time had been lost as the transports, trailing clouds of landing craft, moved to a safer position. But the loading of the landing craft had gone off with amazing smoothness despite the complications. Among the problems was the fact that about half the marines of the first three waves had to be unloaded off the transports into Higgins boats that would carry them to the three LSTs. The Landing Ship, Tank had been designed by John C. Niedermair of the Navy Bureau of Ships in response to a British suggestion a year before Galvanic. They were known in the Navy as "Large Slow Targets" and used, in the Pacific, for transporting everything but tanks. In this case they had carried fifty new amtracs up from Samoa. The marines went on board the LSTs from the Higgins boats and climbed into the virginal amtracs. Finally, like some ungainly sea creature giving birth to living young, the LSTs opened their great bow doors, lowered their ramps, and the loaded amtracs scuttled across the decks and into the water. The rest of the marines of the first three waves boarded the older amtracs directly from the transports.

The evening before, the Japanese sailors on Betio took part in the customary evening ceremony in which they stood facing the emperor's palace and recited the words of the Imperial Rescript that showed the warrior his daily way and reminded him of the glorious reward of *jimbo*, death in battle. As the Imperial Rescript put it: "Be resolved that honor is heavier than the mountains and death lighter than a feather." Many of the men wore *semin bari* around their waists. These cloths, bearing 1,000 red stitches, each sewn by a different person and collected by wives, sisters, and sweethearts standing on street corners in Japan in all kinds of weather, were supposed to provide protection. Perhaps not many of the sailors were convinced of their effectiveness, but, considering the effort that went into their completion, they wore them anyway. Others carried a white silk square with the rising sun emblem and around it legends: "Prayers for your military good fortune," or "I pray for your success in battle." Sometimes they sang *Kimagayo* (the Japanese national anthem):

> The Emperor's reign will last
> For a thousand and then eight thousand generations
> Until pebbles become mighty rocks
> Covered with moss.

And there might be the traditional toast drunk with *Kikumasamune*, ceremonial wine, "It is a good place to die; surely we shall conquer."

By 0430, most of the initial assault force was either in amtracs or on their way to the LSTs. So far there were few signs that the enemy ashore, if indeed there was one, had sighted the invasion fleet. It was almost too good to be true. And it wasn't. A few faint lights on Betio, visible only through binoculars, had gone out. Two hours earlier some of the ships had been illuminated by two powerful searchlights on Betio Island. Signalman John Williams recalls that he and his shipmates on the bridge of the destroyer *Sigsbee*, five miles offshore in the antisubmarine screen, defiantly lit cigarettes while transfixed by the unearthly light since the fact that the "smoking lamp" was out scarcely seemed to matter any more. After a few moments the searchlights turned north and shortly after were turned off, and quiet and the comforting darkness settled down again on the invasion fleet.

Then, at 0441, there was a bright flash beneath the greenish tropical dawn that was just beginning to paint the sky over Betio. A second later the hearts of several thousand men simultaneously skipped a beat as a red star shell curved gracefully up from the island. The mists of secrecy that they had hoped would shield the invasion force had blown away in the winds of dawn over Tarawa Atoll.

2

PRELUDE TO CATASTROPHE

His vitals are overturned,
They are torn apart, they die.
Shame him! Confuse him!
Torture him! Strangle him!
He is finished: he is dead;
He is dead, dead, dead.
He is rotten.

Gilbert Islands death magic.*

As a correspondent for *Le Petit Journal* of Paris wrote, "Thus war has begun, by an act of violence, without previous declaration of war or notification of hostilities; and suddenly and brutally, Japanese guns have set at naught all the efforts of diplomacy, and the hopes of peace-loving people."

That might have been written about Pearl Harbor in December 1941. But it was not. It described the attack of Japanese ships on the Russian fleet as it lay at anchor in the harbor of Port Arthur, Manchuria, at midnight on February 8, 1904. The news of Vice Adm. Heihachiro Togo's† midnight massacre of the Russian Navy thrilled the cadets at the Japanese Naval Academy on Eta Jima Island in Hiroshima Bay. The following year one of them, Isoroku Yamamoto, although still a cadet, participated in the Battle

---

*Reported in *National Geographic*, January 1943.

†In Japanese custom the surname, Togo, would be first. Japanese names in this book are given as they would be in English.

of Tsushima Strait in which the Japanese Navy decisively defeated the Russian fleet. The Russians had lost two battleships and a number of cruisers at Port Arthur. They lost most of the rest of their fleet at Tsushima. Yamamoto had the first two fingers on his left hand severed in that battle. For the rest of his life he wore a glove on that hand even when playing ball with his children, but the minor disfigurement did not handicap his naval career. The injury probably was caused by an exploding gun turret on *Nisshin* on which he served. The accident also disfigured the lower half of his body with more than 120 wounds caused by metal fragments.

Yamamoto was born in Nagaoka in 1884 when his father was fifty-six years old. Isoroku means fifty-six. In 1925 he went to America as a naval attache, and then to London as Japan's representative at the London Naval Conference. Although only five feet three inches tall he was broad-shouldered and barrel-chested. In London he routinely stayed up until 3:00 A.M. playing bridge or poker, rousing his subordinates from bed to play if more accessible partners could not be found. He once asked an apprentice secretary in the Japanese embassy in Washington if he liked to gamble. The flustered young man replied that he had not tried it. Yamamoto answered, "People who don't gamble aren't worth talking to." But he didn't drink. While still a young officer he had gotten so drunk near the Japanese Naval Academy at Eta Jima that he fell into a ditch and passed out. From that time on he never touched alcoholic beverages.

He traveled widely in America in 1935. And he, like most Japanese naval officers, got along well with his American counterparts. The Japanese officers were, as one American admiral put it, "mostly gentlemen, a very different breed from the narrow-minded boors who commanded the Japanese Army."

Despite his enthusiasm for gambling, Yamamoto was not reckless. The biographical card on him in the Office of Naval Intelligence in Washington described him as "exceptionally able, forceful, a man of quick thinking." The biographical note went on to point out that he was an habitual winner at poker and was the Go champion of the Imperial Navy. Success at both games is the result of careful, analytical thinking, not impetuous plunges.

In 1939 Isoroku Yamamoto, fifty-five years old and now an admiral, was sent to sea as commander in chief of the *rengo kantai* (the Japanese Combined Fleet).* At that point, he had four children from a loveless

---

*The Imperial Combined Fleet was made up of the First Fleet (Battle Force) of three battleship divisions (three ships each), two cruiser divisions (three ships each), and two destroyer divisions (fourteen destroyers and a light cruiser each); Second Fleet (Scouting) of four cruiser and two destroyer divisions; Third Fleet (Blockade and Transport), four cruisers and twelve destroyers; the Fourth and Fifth fleets (seven cruisers and ten destroyers in all); Sixth Fleet (Submarines), three light cruisers and forty-two submarines; First Air Fleet, five carrier divisions (nine carriers total); and the Combined Air Fleet (land-based) consisting of various units based in Japan, Formosa, Indochina, and elsewhere.

marriage, and for five years he had been the lover of the geisha Chioko Kawai who worked under the professional name of Umeryu ("Plum Dragon"). They had met and fallen in love in 1934, and she remained his mistress for the last ten years of his life. Yamamoto was described by his associates as taciturn, meticulous, kind, and trustworthy. Admiral Yamamoto was a man who kept his promises. He was sent to sea in 1939 to save his life.

In the 1920s, there arose in Japan the Oriental version of Nazism called *Kodo-Ha,* the Way of the Emperor. Its adherents were called Koda men. Their program called for nationalization of property; domination of the government by the Army; abolition of democratic institutions; and liberation of other Asians in India, China, the Phillipines, and elsewhere in the Pacific basin from oppression, that is, domination by non-Orientals. As in Germany, a struggle began between liberal and fascist elements for the control of Japan. It did not end until October 1941, just several weeks before Pearl Harbor.

Assassination was a favorite tactic of the Koda men. In 1932 the minister of finance and the prime minister were killed, and there were plans to assassinate the American ambassador to Japan, Joseph Grew; and Charlie Chaplin, then visiting Tokyo. The object was to provoke war with the United States, thus assuring military control of the Japanese government. When Yamamoto was navy vice-minister one of his colleagues said to him: "I hear you're getting lots of threatening letters." Yamamoto replied, "Yes, some of the worst of them even announce that they're going to do me in the next day. But killing me isn't going to change the navy's thinking. I'm sure my successor would say just the same things."

More assassinations of ministers followed even though some of the victims held high military rank. On September 18, 1931, the Japanese Army in Korea had invaded Manchuria on a pretext, and without the government's permission. This was an example of *gekokujo* (a sort of "divine insubordination").* Two colonels (Koda men) were using the Japanese Kwantung Army as their own private force, and although the Army General Staff ordered them to stop, they didn't stop. Nothing was ever done about it because the army itself was riven into two factions, and neither was strong enough to control the other.

Junior officers in both services could, and did, exercise *gekokujo,* over-riding commands from their superiors who, if they disagreed, were in danger of assassination.

The invasion of her Manchurian province automatically provoked a state of war with China. This in turn meant that the military assumed constitutional control of the Japanese government. The government con-

---

*The word dates from the fifteenth century when provincial lords refused to obey the *shogun,* the "de facto ruler." The emperor was a mere puppet.

tinued to announce its desire for peace in East Asia, but what it meant was summarized in the Koda version of *Mein Kampf*: "a feudal peace obtained by the emergence of the strongest country [that is, Japan], which will dominate all others of the world." On July 7, 1937 Japan similarly invaded other parts of China after another trumped-up incident. Although the American man in the street may have felt sorry for the Chinese, particularly after the atrocities committed by Japanese soldiers in Nanking were publicized, he took the reasonable position that if the Chinese could not defend themselves against the Japanese whom they outnumbered six to one there wasn't much that anyone else could do either.

In December of that year Japanese planes sank the U.S. gunboat *Panay* on the Yangtze River in an unprovoked attack; then the Japanese machine-gunned the officers and men who had made it to shore. A few days later Naval Intelligence learned that the attack on the *Panay* had been planned by an officer on the carrier *Kaga*. Subsequently, there were several hundred other "incidents" in which American missions were attacked by the Japanese between 1937 and 1941 until the Chinese were themselves saying that the most dangerous place to be in an air raid was at an American mission. Prince Fumimaro Konoye, a liberal, was then the Japanese premier, but he was unable to restrain the militarists.

Under the Japanese Constitution of 1889, the emperor alone determined the size of the armed forces, and the military controlled the government in periods of national emergency. Thus, the military could gain control of the government almost whenever it chose. The system had worked well for the militarists. In the 1884-85 war with China, Japan won Formosa. Ten years later, she defeated Russia. In 1910, Japan annexed Korea. Four years after that, she entered the First World War on the side of Britain and France (three years before the United States did) in order to obtain the German colonies in the Far East. Among these were the German concession of Tsingtao on the coast of China; the Marianas except for Guam, ceded to the United States by Spain in 1898, and the Caroline and Marshall islands. As early as 1915 the government of Japan made it clear to the Chinese that it considered China as under its "protection."

The Japanese Diet put a stop to military adventures for a period of less than ten years after 1922. During this time the Japanese government returned Tsingtao to China and accepted the multinational Naval Limitation and Reduction Treaty. It joined with the United States and seven other powers to guarantee the sovereignty and territorial integrity of China. She also signed the Kellogg-Briand Pact outlawing war ("peace by incantation" as Samuel Eliot Morison described it).

In 1924, the Japanese were excluded from the possibility of immigration to the United States. The Japanese had voluntarily agreed in 1907 that they would not allow their nationals to emmigrate to the United States even though they could legally have done so. They naturally regarded the 1924 exclusion as a gratuitous insult, and the long period of U.S.-Japanese friendship began to wither away. The 1930 London Naval Limitation and Reduction Treaty violated the right of the emperor alone to determine the size of his armed forces, and the Japanese military were furious. That the treaty had many advantages for Japan was easily obscured by emphasis on the slogan "5-5-3" (the ratio of capital ships possessed by the United States, Britain, and Japan). It became a Japanese jingoist chant like the nineteenth-century American cries of "54-40 or fight" and "Remember the Maine," all of which were widely accepted substitutes for thinking.

Later, when Japan abrogated the Naval Limitation and Reduction Treaty, Yamamoto said: "It's very regrettable that the Washington and London treaties should be done away with. I see nothing wrong with the 5-5-3 ratio." Yamamoto, a realist, could see that for the United States and Britain, facing a two-ocean war, the ratio was unfavorable vis-à-vis Japan who could concentrate her forces in the Pacific. Under the treaty the United States had forsworn building up any of its bases west of Pearl Harbor (Guam, Midway, and the Philippines), while Britain agreed not to strengthen those east of Singapore and north of Australia. In June 1938 Great Britain, France, and the United States signed a protocol raising the limit of battleship tonnage from 35,000 to 45,000 tons, thus making way for the *Iowa* class, but Japan, in great secrecy, had already laid down the 63,700-ton *Musashi* and *Yamato*. For the United States the "treaty strength" authorized in 1934 would not be attained until 1944, a year before the end of the Second World War.

This delay in U.S. naval growth was due to a combination of economic depression, pacifism, and the exhortations of Gen. William Mitchell, known to the gullible journalists who flocked around him as "Billy." Those causes suppressed U.S. naval development until just a few years before Pearl Harbor.

Prince Konoye sent a secret message to President Franklin Roosevelt on January 23, 1941. It read in part, "The Japanese would rather lose the war in China than lose the domestic war to their own extremists. . . . They [the Japanese majority] feel that if some constructive cooperation is not realized with the United States before March or April, the Fascist element will take control in . . . Japan." And it did. In response to continued air raids by the Japanese on American missions and churches in China, President Roosevelt had imposed economic sanctions on Japan on July 26, 1940. He had the strong support of the American people (who generally did not realize that the consequence probably would be war with Japan).

On April 13, 1941 Russia and Japan concluded a nonaggression pact. This freed Russia to concentrate on the threat from Germany (troops from Siberia later repulsed the German advance at the gates of Moscow), and Japan could pour troops southward from Manchuria. On July 2 the Japanese government called up between one and two million conscripts and pulled its merchant ships out of the Atlantic. Three weeks later, on July 25, she announced that the Vichy government of France (set up to collaborate with the Germans) had consented to admit Japan as a joint "protector" of French Indochina. Thus Japan could expand militarily throughout that entire colony (now Vietnam, Laos, and Cambodia) enhancing her menace to the Philippines and Malaya.

Roosevelt found this unbearable. He quickly froze Japanese assets in the United States and shut off oil exports to Japan. From that moment, war with Japan became inevitable, barring either of two veritable miracles. Either the Japanese would have to withdraw from China and renounce their advance into Southeast Asia, or the United States and its allies would have to relent on their embargoes and acquiesce in further Japanese conquests.

At an imperial conference on September 6, 1941, the General Staff's contingency plan for military operations against the United States was discussed. It was not the first time. Whether diplomacy or military action was to prevail was unresolved, and the military chiefs remained silent when the question was raised. Then, for the first time in memory, and to the amazement of everyone, the emperor spoke in an imperial conference: "We regret deeply that the high command has not seen fit to clarify [this] question. Our august ancestor, Meiji Tenno, once wrote a poem which we are going to read to you now—

> All the seas everywhere
> are brothers one to another.
> Why then do the winds and waves of strife
> rage so violently through the world?

We have read this poem over and over again, and we are determined to make the Meiji ideal of peace prevail in the world." The meeting adjourned, as Prince Konoye later wrote, "in an atmosphere of unprecedented tension."

Although the emperor had spoken strongly for peace, provocations against the United States continued. Throughout 1941 American churches, hospitals, schools, and universities in China were bombed by Japanese planes despite the flag markings on their roofs.

Still later, his first efforts blocked by the American State Department under Cordell Hull, Konoye tried again to arrange a meeting with Roosevelt. The overture came to naught. On the morning of September 18, 1941, four men armed with guns, daggers, and short ceremonial swords attacked Premier Konoye as he was leaving his home, Tekigaiso Villa, in the quiet Tokyo suburb of Ogikubo. The attackers were overpowered by the prince's police guard, but the attack was a clear warning. A little more than a week later the Tripartite (or Axis) Pact was signed in Berlin, allying Japan, Germany, and Italy.

For three more months the forces on both sides that opposed war between Japan and the United States strove mightily and sincerely to prevent it. Negotiations were frequently hampered rather than helped by the fact that U.S. cryptographers had broken the Japanese diplomatic code. Truculent messages, made more menacing by inept translation, kept crossing Cordell Hull's desk. One, transmitted late in 1941, was translated as saying: "This proposal is our revised ultimatum." What the Japanese had actually written was: "This is our proposal setting forth what are virtually our final concessions," a message with a very different meaning.

By the end of September 1941 the Japanese oil supply had dwindled to fifteen million barrels. The army had set a deadline of six weeks, beginning on September 6, for negotiations to be completed with the United States. After that, Japan would have to go to war to secure oil in Southeast Asia. The president of the Japanese national planning board had said that he could increase domestic production of oil and other materials for a fraction of what a Pacific war would cost. The militarists rejected this course. Only by a world war could Tojo and the men of *Kodo-Ha* complete their control of Japan. When their deadline passed without result Konoye resigned and the Tojo Cabinet was formed on October 18. Tojo became minister of war and home secretary, and remained chief of the Army General Staff. The domination by the militarists was complete. General Tojo, far more moderate than many of his colleagues, promptly extended the deadline for agreement with the United States for an additional six weeks, to November 25. Proposals and counterproposals flew back and forth across the Pacific as Yamamoto's Pearl Harbor striking force sailed north and General Marshall prepared to send an additional 21,000 American troops to the Philippines. He planned to send them on December 8, 1941!

From the decoded cables the Americans knew that Tojo was poised to strike—but where? On the basis of ship movements the most likely spot seemed to be somewhere in Southeast Asia—the Philippines, Thailand, Malaya, or Borneo. Yamamoto's force in the stormy North Pacific had not been noticed.

Admiral Yamamoto had bitterly opposed the Tripartite Pact as well as Japan's going to war with the United States. For this he was detested by the men of *Kodo-Ha*. Expecting possible assassination, he wrote his will in 1939. In that same year, the government sent him to sea as commander in chief to protect him from the guns and knives of the extremists.

Yamamoto was well aware that the immense industrial strength of America would prove decisive in any long war. As he told Prince Konoye: "If we are ordered to do it (make war on America), then I can guarantee to put up a tough fight for the first six months, but I have absolutely no confidence as to what would happen if it went on for two or three years.... I hope at least that you'll make every effort to avoid war with America."

But when war with America became inevitable, Yamamoto loyally devised Combined Fleet Secret Operation Order Number 1, on November 5, 1941. It was the best plan he could develop to bring the war to a speedy conclusion, although a few days later he wrote to an old friend: "I find my present position extremely odd—obliged to make up my mind to and pursue unswervingly a course that is precisely the opposite of my personal views." The burden of carrying out Yamamoto's plan and the parallel designs of the army commanders fell on the men of the Japanese armed forces supported by Japanese civilians who worked nine to twelve hours a day, with two days off each month.

The training the Japanese military men received was brutal and effective beyond the wildest dreams of even the most sadistic U.S. Marine Corps drill instructor. Former Ambassador to Japan Joseph C. Grew tells of American Army observers watching a Japanese regiment on maneuvers. The Japanese commander took his men on a twenty-nine hour march without rest. Some of the men fell asleep while marching, one officer ran into a pile of lumber. On reaching their goal the exhausted men were put to setting up defensive positions and sending out patrols. One American officer asked why the men, obviously close to collapse, could not be allowed a little sleep. The Japanese commander replied, "My men know how to sleep already. I am training them to learn to stay awake." The Japanese infantryman trained fourteen hours a day, six days a week. He might march twenty-five miles a day for weeks carrying two-thirds his own weight. Such marches ended with a run to prove that the men still had reserves of strength. It was little wonder that the Japanese fighting man, so vigorously trained and further hardened by a decade of combat in Manchuria and China, became widely regarded as a superman.

Sailors had it no better. Japanese ships carried many more men than an American ship of the same size, 692 men on a heavy cruiser, for example, versus 517 on a comparable American ship. And, as a Japanese Navy pamphlet of 1937 pointed out, the fleet left their home ports in late January for intensive training in the cold and stormy arctic waters with only two or three days at anchor after a month of operation. "There are no Saturdays or Sundays, especially when under way, where one drill follows another—literally a period of no rest and no sleep. This is because if we are not under way we cannot carry out actual battle training, and so with a tenacious and tireless spirit we are striving to reach a superhuman degree of skill and perfect fighting efficiency." In these exercises, the Combined Fleet would lose fifty to one hundred men swept overboard or otherwise killed, but Japanese newspapers were forbidden to mention it. It was from those icy, storm-lashed waters that Yamamoto launched his attack on Pearl Harbor.

For thirty-two years the General Staff of the Imperial Japanese Navy devised annual fleet problems around its basic strategic concepts. Each year the goal was the same: destruction of the U.S. Pacific Fleet.

The U.S. Navy did fleet problems, too. In the fall of 1932 the problem devised by Adm. Frank Scofield, commander in chief of the Pacific Fleet, on the eve of his retirement, included an enemy attack on Pearl Harbor. When the problem was put to the test the American "defending" forces failed to detect the "aggressor" forces, which broke through and successfully "attacked" Pearl Harbor. After Admiral Scofield's retirement the fervor created in the U.S. Navy by this result quietly died away (although in Fleet Problem XIX, in 1939, *Saratoga* launched a successful surprise mock bombing raid on Pearl Harbor from a point 100 miles away, using the same tactics employed by the Japanese three years later), but the idea remained thoroughly fixed in the mind of Isoroku Yamamoto.

Part One of Yamamoto's "Secret Operation Order Number One" was the attack on the ninety-four ships in Pearl Harbor by 360 Japanese carrier planes that morning of December 7, 1941; it was to be carried out thirty minutes *after* a formal declaration of war had been delivered to the American government. That such prior notification did not occur was due to the fact that only an inept typist could be found in the Japanese embassy in Washington to transcribe the long cable into a form suitable for presentation to Cordell Hull.

The Pearl Harbor strike force sailed on November 26. American Naval Intelligence, later to score many notable coups, completely lost track of the Japanese carriers. On December 1 the call letters for all ships in the Japanese Navy were changed, four days later, the highest priority Japanese naval code was changed as well, and the carriers maintained strict radio silence.

On December 1 the emperor's seal was affixed to the document declaring war, and the next day Adm. Chuichi Nagumo received the crucial message: *"Niitaka yama nobore"* ("Climb Mount Niitaka") authorizing the attack. Nevertheless, the strike could be called off at any point before the planes were actually in the air. The fighters and dive-bombers did not have radios (signals were by flares), and those in the bombers were tuned to a Honolulu radio station for homing in on Pearl Harbor. When Nagumo sailed he thought that six American carriers might be at Pearl Harbor. He only later learned that *Saratoga* was in San Diego and that Japanese intelligence had failed to discover that *Hornet* and *Yorktown* were in the Atlantic! He much later learned that *Lexington* ("Lady Lex," as she was affectionately called) and *Enterprise* were at sea. Had they not been, the course of the Pacific war might have been very different.

The planes with the rising sun emblem fell out of the sky onto Pearl Harbor like ravening hawks on a chicken yard.

And the attack spread devastation among the massed battleships at Ford Island and the planes at Hickam Field. Pearl Harbor is the legendary abode of the Polynesian shark goddess *Kaahupahau*, and viewing the carnage, it was hard not to believe that supernatural forces had been involved. Of the eight battleships at Pearl Harbor only three escaped serious damage. Only thirty Army and no Navy fighters got into the air. In addition to ships sunk and damaged, the attack destroyed or badly damaged 347 planes and killed or wounded nearly 3,600 persons. The Japanese lost twenty-nine planes, one large and five midget submarines.

But the Japanese pilots, whose orders were to concentrate on battleships

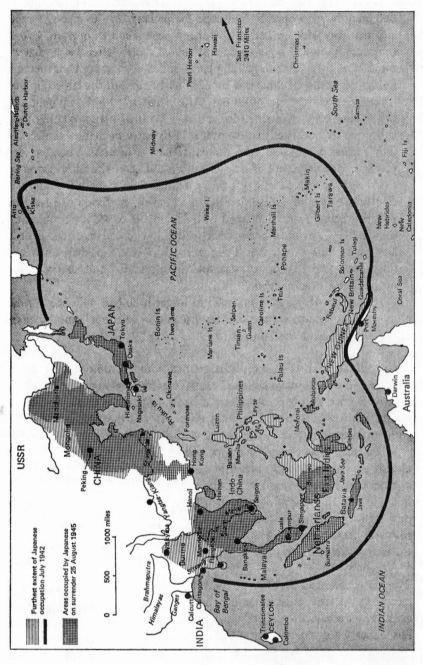

The Pacific Theater

and aircraft, ignored several important targets. The attacking pilots missed the row upon row of fuel tanks containing forty-five million barrels of oil that supplied the motive power for the Pacific Fleet, as well as the machine shops and dry docks needed for ship repair. Even though they attacked from the southeast, a route that took them right over the navy yard, the submarine docks, and the tank farm, they obediently passed them by. After returning to their carriers, Japanese pilots pleaded for a chance to go back to destroy the oil tanks. Had this vast reserve been destroyed, the U.S. Navy might have been forced to withdraw to the Pacific coast and leave Hawaii undefended. But the Japanese pilots were overruled. The Americans at Pearl Harbor could be expected to put up a stiff fight if they were attacked again, and Japanese plane losses would be heavy. Moreover, the carrier task force would be jeopardized by staying too long in the vicinity and Admiral Nagumo judged his ships too important to risk.

In Japanese eyes Pearl Harbor was not the most important part of Top Secret Operation Order No. One. What mattered was acquisition of raw materials. As Yamamoto put it in Order No. One when it was issued to the Combined Fleet on November 5, 1941: "When Britain and America have been driven from the Netherlands Indies and the Philippines, an independent, self-supporting economic entity will be firmly established. The vast and far-reaching fundamental principle, the goal of our nation— *Hakko Ichiu* (bringing the eight corners of the world under one roof)— will be demonstrated to the world." Still, the first step in Yamamoto's overall plan appeared to be a great success. On December 7, 1941, Japan's ally, Germany, controlled most of Europe, had isolated England, was threatening the Suez Canal, and had pushed the Russian Army back to Stalingrad. In the early months of 1942, Japanese troops spread out over Southeast Asia, extended their control of China, and took Hong Kong, Singapore, the Philippines, and most of Burma. Japanese forces then struck south until they controlled nearly all the islands between the Asian continent and the very edge of Australia and extended their control as far east as the international date line. In February 1942, 243 Japanese carrier planes had demolished Darwin, Australia. The stepping stone for the proposed Japanese invasion of Australia would be Port Moresby, New Guinea, only 300 miles from Australia's northern tip.

The Battle of the Java Sea, in late January 1942, was the greatest sea battle since Jutland and the greatest Allied disaster since Pearl Harbor. At 1:00 P.M. on February 27, 1942, four cruisers and fourteen destroyers of the Japanese Fifth Fleet encountered five Allied cruisers and nine destroyers. Of the original Allied fleet, only four American destroyers returned to Australia. The Japanese lost no ships.

Japan's inner fortress (the home islands, China north of the Yangtze River, Korea, and Manchuria) was virtually self-sustaining. The ancient slogan of *Hakko Ichiu*, was coming close to reality.

The Japanese now controlled an area that, although largely water, was as large as that conquered by Genghis Khan and his Golden Horde in the fourteenth century. It was an area much greater than that commanded by either Alexander the Great or by Rome at the height of its glory. If, as planned, the Japanese conquered China, one-half of mankind would live under their rule.

In the spring of 1942, Hitler also ruled an empire larger than the United States, and American merchant ships were being torpedoed at the rate of three or four a day in the Atlantic. Admiral Ernest J. King, commander in chief of the U.S. Navy and chief of Naval Operations, had to transfer *Yorktown*, four light cruisers, and two destroyer squadrons to the Atlantic on April 4, 1942 to deal with the submarine menace. The night before this transfer, a U-boat wolf pack had sunk ten of the twenty-two ships in a slow Atlantic convoy. In 1942 Adm. Karl Doenitz's U-boats sank more than 1,000 merchantmen in the Arctic and Atlantic oceans (5.7 million tons of shipping), and by July, the Germans were completing a U-boat every day while the Allies were sinking only slightly more than one a month (sixteen during the entire year).

Admiral Yamamoto was convinced that, with the vast amount of territory she had captured, Japan was now not only self-sufficient but invincible. Japan, he counseled, should now insist upon peace with the United States. Even before Pearl Harbor the Japanese fleet outnumbered the Allied naval vessels in the Pacific by more than two to one. Now it seemed that the United States—with the cream of its Navy rusting beneath the waves at Pearl Harbor, and with only a tiny cadre of trained soldiers, sailors, and marines—was in no position to resist a peace offer.

Yamamoto's assessment may have been correct. But Japan's militarists had achieved success beyond their dreams. In just three months they had taken territory that they had estimated would require twice as long. Moreover, their victories were cheaply bought. Even by May 1942, after six months of the Pacific war, Japan had lost only twenty-three naval vessels, none larger than a destroyer, in addition to a few hundred planes and a few thousand men; she had new ships joining the fleet that more than made up for the losses. Japan had also lost 300,000 tons of merchant shipping. But in the single month of May 1942 Allied losses of merchant ships were twice that; March of 1943 was equally bad. On land, the results of the Japanese campaigns were similarly impressive. The conquest of Malaya, which ended with the fall of Singapore, cost the Japanese Army fewer than 10,000 casualties against 138,708 for the British. In the Central Pacific, Truk in the Carolines, Saipan in the Marianas, and Kwajalein in the Marshalls were each the center of a Japanese defensive system easily supported from Japan. No U.S. search plane could reach them from available bases. The range of the B-24 was 1,100 miles, even the nearest of the Marshall Islands was that distance from Guadalcanal, and Kwajalein was farther still.

Admiral Tadaichi Hara, the carrier commander at the Battle of the Coral Sea wrote that the results of the Japanese successes, "caused many officials in high places to succumb to the so-called 'Victory Disease'." A major symptom of the disease was the belief that such rapid victories could be achieved again and again and that the Allies, particularly the Americans, were powerless to prevent them.

For months there had been little the American armed forces could do but lick their wounds, make occasional raids of largely symbolic significance, and watch with grudging admiration as the Japanese steamroller moved inexorably south, east, and west over the Pacific basin, crushing all opposition. But on the American home front there were developments that boded ill for General Tojo and his friends. Destroyer production in the United States had been only slightly more than one a month in 1941, despite the gathering clouds of war. In 1943, nearly eleven new destroyers slid down the ways every thirty days. On December 7, 1941, total naval personnel (Navy, Marine Corps, and Coast Guard) were slightly more than 420,000. By the end of 1943 that number would approach three million.

Then, in May 1942, as the Japanese warlords were wallowing in mutual self-esteem, a Japanese fleet of three carriers and their escorts of cruisers and destroyers was confronted with an equally impressive American armada centered around the carriers *Lexington* and *Yorktown* in the sea northwest of Australia. The meeting was no accident. Lieutenant Commander Joseph J. Rochefort, a former enlisted man, then chief of the Fourteenth Naval District Combat Intelligence Unit in Pearl Harbor, had broken the Japanese naval codes. He and his 120-man team, including the entire band of the sunken battleship *California,* worked nearly round the clock in a windowless basement in the navy yard protected by vaultlike steel doors, steel-barred gates, and ever-present armed guards. Rochefort knew where the Japanese fleet would be, and the U.S. Navy elected to meet them.

It was entirely a battle of carrier-based planes against ships, the first in history. Neither surface force ever sighted the other. When the Battle of the Coral Sea was over, Lady Lex had gone to the bottom; *Yorktown* was severely damaged. The Japanese had lost their light carrier *Shoho,* many of their carrier aircraft, and their carriers *Shokaku* and *Zuikaku* were damaged. From the standpoint of ship losses, it was probably a Japanese victory, and it had been won by the Japanese Fifth Air Squadron, generally regarded by the Japanese as the worst in the fleet. If the Fifth Air Squadron beat the best the Americans had to offer, what would their betters accomplish? Or, as the other Japanese carrier pilots put it, "Son of concubine gained a victory, so sons of legal wives should find no rival in the world." But the power of the Imperial Japanese Fleet to support a landing against a vital Allied base at Port Moresby, New Guinea, had been dissipated.

A month later, in June, the world's mightiest battleship left Japan and sailed east. *Yamato*, Admiral Yamamoto's flagship was, with her sister ship, *Musashi,* the pride of the Hiroshima naval shipyard where they were built. They were the only battleships in the world with eighteen-inch guns.

Yamato had been commissioned only weeks before the attack on Pearl Harbor. She was now part of a massive Japanese force of five carriers, three battleships, fourteen cruisers, fifty-eight destroyers, seventeen submarines, and twenty supporting vessels. These other ships included transports carrying the force that was to seize from the Americans Midway Island, some 1,600 miles west of Hawaii. It was Admiral Yamamoto's next great operation after the attack on Pearl Harbor. But Yamamoto's armada sailed into a trap, again made possible by the broken codes.

The Japanese had been scheduled to change their codes before the Midway battle; such a change always blinded the U.S. Navy's Combat Intelligence Unit at Pearl Harbor until the new code could be broken. But the invasion of Midway had caused so much extra work that there had not been time to change the codes and, besides, the Japanese were convinced that their codes were unbreakable. It was June 2, not the originally scheduled May 1, before the codes were changed, and by then the Midway striking force was already at sea. The jaws of the snare were the carriers *Enterprise, Hornet,* and the battered *Yorktown* (fresh from repairs at Pearl Harbor), along with thirteen cruisers, twenty-seven destroyers, and a dozen other vessels.

The crew of *Yorktown* had been looking forward to two months in a West Coast shipyard. Instead, shipfitters, welders, and the like were flown out to her as she steamed toward Pearl Harbor licking her wounds from the Coral Sea. After forty-eight frantic hours in the Pearl Harbor Navy Yard, *Yorktown* steamed back into battle! Again, losses were heavy on both sides. Gallant *Yorktown* went to the bottom of the Pacific. Japan, however, lost the cream of her navy pilots, 350 planes, four carriers, a heavy cruiser, and 3,500 men. It was the first defeat the Japanese Navy had suffered in 350 years.

Midway and the Battle of the Coral Sea dealt crushing blows to the Japanese Naval Air Force and to the Imperial Navy. Isoroku Yamamoto had said that the war with the United States must end before the beginning of 1943, otherwise America's industrial might would begin to tip the balance against the emperor's forces. Now Yamamoto, aboard his flagship, led his battered fleet back to Japan. An air officer described him as dazed and glassy-eyed. "He sat sipping rice gruel helplessly on the forward bridge." With six months to go before the end of 1942, Japanese prospects looked far less cheerful than they had even a month before.

In 1942, the U.S. Army in the southwest Pacific under General Douglas MacArthur had begun the slow and agonizing task of removing the Japanese forces from the vast island of New Guinea where they posed a strong threat to Australia. On June 24 Adm. Ernest King ordered Adm. Chester Nimitz, commander in chief of the Pacific Fleet, to seize Tulagi, a small island northeast of Guadalcanal, and Guadalcanal itself, by amphibious assault on August 1, only five weeks later. The Japanese, now planning to attack Port Moresby overland, needed the airfield on Guadalcanal to ward off Allied forces coming from the east and south. When the airfield was discovered, in June 1942, King instantly realized that this could not be allowed to happen although the time remaining to prevent it was pitifully short. King intended that Nimitz intrude into territory assigned to MacArthur's command and he did so without consulting either the president or the Joint Chiefs of Staff (JCS). The next day he asked the JCS for their concurrence. Surprisingly, MacArthur agreed that it was a sensible plan, and after a few days of agonizing, Gen. George Marshall, chief of staff of the Army, and King simply moved the line separating the Army and Navy commands in the South Pacific so that Nimitz's command now embraced the Solomon Islands, of which Guadalcanal was a part.

In August 1942, the First Marine Division waded ashore on Guadalcanal to begin the battle. The landing was virtually unopposed. It was two weeks after the landing on Guadalcanal before the first important land battle took place at the Tenaru (Ilu) River. (The river the marines called the Ilu was the Tenaru, and vice versa, but the error was not discovered, or at least not taken seriously, until after the campaign was over.) More trouble came later when the Japanese vigorously reinforced their troops on the island and supported them with periodic air and naval attacks. The Second Marine Division was called into the fray as were elements of an Army division. The accompanying naval battles were disastrous for the United States. The Battle of Savo Island, on August 9, 1942, was begun by Rear Adm. Gunichi Mikawa with one light and five heavy cruisers and a division of destroyers. This action reduced Allied strength in heavy cruisers by more than one-third. Four were sunk, one damaged. As Admiral King remarked: "That, as far as I was concerned, was the blackest day of the war." The only bright spot was that Admiral Mikawa withdrew without attacking the transports loaded with supplies for the marines on the 'Canal. If those supplies had been destroyed the position of the marines on the island would rapidly have become untenable.

Still, most of the American battleships had been lost at Pearl Harbor, most of the aircraft carriers lost or severely damaged in the Coral Sea, and then many heavy cruisers were lost in the Battle of Savo Island. At the conclusion of that naval encounter the Japanese held Guadalcanal in the palm of their hand, ripe for squeezing. Fortunately, they let the opportunity slip through their fingers. By autumn 1942 only the *Saratoga*, *Enterprise*, and *Ranger* were afloat of the seven carriers the United States had had on December 7, 1941.

Before the campaign for Guadalcanal was over it had cost the U.S. Navy twenty-four ships, including two carriers and eight cruisers, in addition to those damaged.

Five months later, in January 1943, Guadalcanal was declared secure by American forces. Then the First and Second Marine divisions, or what was left of them, were sent off to Australia and New Zealand, respectively, to rest and refit for their next operation. For the Second Marine Division, that

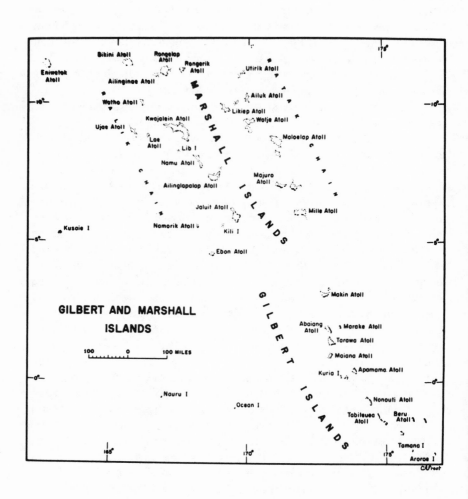

GILBERT AND MARSHALL
ISLANDS

100 — 0 — 100 MILES

operation would be the invasion of Tarawa Atoll. At this point, seventy-five percent of the survivors of the First Division had active or latent malaria, as did half of the Second Division, in addition to widespread dengue (bone-break) fever and the ubiquitous jungle rot, an often severe fungal infection.

The Battles of Midway and the Coral Sea had been aimed at blunting a Japanese offensive. The actions of MacArthur in New Guinea were also part of what Admiral King called the defensive-offensive phase. Admiral King had explained on November 30, 1942 that the earlier defensive phase was like that of a boxer covered up; the defensive-offensive phase was similar to that of a boxer covering up while looking for an opportunity to counterpunch; the offensive-defensive phase was analogous to blocking punches with one hand while hitting with the other; and, finally, the offensive phase was like that of a boxer hitting with both hands. In the case of New Guinea the goal of the defensive-offensive phase was that of securing Australia from immediate attack. This was consistent with the basic strategic decision reached at the Anglo-American conference in Washington on March 27, 1941. The agreement resulting from this meeting said, "The Atlantic and European area is considered to be the decisive theatre. . . . If Japan does enter the war, the military strategy in the Far East will be defensive."

Germany was regarded as the first Allied priority even before Pearl Harbor because she was thought to have a far greater military potential than Japan. Germany already controlled almost the entire Atlantic coast of Europe and threatened the Americas. England was already fighting Germany and could be assisted immediately while only China was fighting Japan and supplies could not reach the Chinese mainland.

Now, with the Battles of the Coral Sea and Midway over and Guadalcanal in Allied hands, Admiral King and his Pacific commander, Adm. Chester A. Nimitz, could think of what to do next to secure their supply lines to Australia and New Zealand and to prepare for moving northward up the Pacific island chains toward Japan.

The Battle of Midway greatly accelerated the need for a strong blow against the Japanese in the Pacific. In May 1942 both MacArthur and Nimitz now appreciated the great power of aircraft carriers and each wanted the bulk of those available to be under his own command. So the basic question was whether MacArthur with carrier and Marine components should mount the first offensive up the Papuan Peninsula toward Rabaul, or whether a Navy officer, who might be expected to be more considerate of carrier vulnerability, should move from the South Pacific area into the southeastern Solomons. Only a limited offensive was possible. Not even that could be undertaken unless carriers could support the attack with relative safety.

At that time, in early 1943, the Japanese occupied the western half of southern New Guinea, all of the Netherlands East Indies extending 3,000 miles west to Sabang in the Indian Ocean, all of the Philippines, British Borneo, the Malay States and Straits Settlements (including Singapore), French Indochina, Thailand, the Andaman and Nicobar islands in the Indian Ocean, all of Burma except for a few square miles of razorback northern ridges, much of the interior of China, and all but two of its deep-water ports. The East China Sea was a Japanese lake; it would be eighteen months before an Allied aircraft would cross it. Four American carriers had been sunk (*Lexington, Yorktown, Hornet,* and *Wasp*), *Enterprise* had been on continuous duty for two full years and had sustained bomb damage twice, *Ranger* was in the Atlantic. Only *Saratoga* was in the Pacific in full fighting trim.

It was not an easy decision for King and Nimitz since the balance of naval power in the Pacific was still delicate. Production of new U.S. Navy planes and pilots was barely balancing losses, a greater replacement pool had to be accumulated, and the demands on the Navy for the invasion of North Africa in November 1942 were an additional burden.

In the Pacific, the southwest region was under the command of Gen. Douglas MacArthur whose goal it was to fight his way up the islands of the western Pacific to the Philippines from which he had recently been ejected by the Japanese advance. The second spearhead, under the command of Adm. William F. "Bull" Halsey, was to move up the islands of the eastern Pacific until it merged with MacArthur's forces for the final assault on the Japanese homelands. MacArthur, although he had agreed to it, regarded the dominant Navy role in the invasion of Guadalcanal as simply a further extension of the plot for "the complete absorption of the national defense function by the Navy" that he had "accidentally" uncovered when he was chief of staff. His agreement was, moreover, completely out of keeping with his request that he be given several Marine units and carriers to further his own plans. But whatever MacArthur's feelings, Bull Halsey was raring to go. As he put it, "Before we're through with them, the Japanese language will be spoken only in hell." At the point of Admiral Halsey's spearhead was the tiny island of Betio in Tarawa Atoll.

The Gilbert Islands, of which Tarawa Atoll is part, consist of some sixteen atolls straddling the equator just west of the international date line. The islands were discovered by a Portuguese navigator in 1616 and named for a British shipmaster, Thomas Gilbert, in 1788. Lieutenant Charles Wilkes of the U.S. Navy, as commodore of the United States Exploring Expedition, had visited the Gilberts in 1841 with his ships *Peacock* and *Flying Fish,* and it was Wilkes' chart of Tarawa Atoll on which the invasion forces largely depended more than a century later. Three days after Pearl Harbor, at 0100, the enterprising Japanese left a token force on Tarawa Atoll from the destroyers *Yunagi* and *Asanagi,* set up a seaplane base on Makin (pronounced Muckin or Muggin) a hundred miles to the north, and established coast watchers on other atolls of the Gilberts to report on Allied ship movements.

At this point, Tarawa was a minor nuisance to the U.S. Navy. Then, in August 1942, a grotesque blunder converted the sleepy atoll into a major threat to the U.S. supply lines to Australia. At the time the action—a minor tactical success but a strategic catastrophe—was seen as an act of great daring. And it was.

President Franklin Delano Roosevelt was enchanted with the activities of the British commandos. As early as June 1940 he had forced a reluctant Marine Corps to set up similar units, the Raider battalions. Marine Commandant Maj. Gen. Thomas Holcomb had felt that every marine had training equivalent to that of the commandos and that, therefore, no special forces were necessary.

On August 17, 1942 Lt. Col. Evans F. Carlson's Second Marine Raider Battalion, accompanied by the president's son, Maj. James Roosevelt, as second in command, landed on Makin from the submarines *Nautilus* and *Argonaut* and made a spectacular attack. It drew Japanese attention away from Guadalcanal. It made favorable, if inaccurate, headlines at a time when cheerful headlines were hard to find in U.S. newspapers. It gave Marine Corps morale a boost. And it greatly multiplied the number of marine bodies that floated in the surf off Tarawa's beaches fifteen months later.

News of the Makin raid swiftly reached the Navy Building just outside the moat of the Imperial Palace grounds in Tokyo and it was quickly passed on to *Dai Honei,* Imperial Headquarters. The Imperial General Staff met to consider the significance of the Makin raid. All agreed that it presaged an invasion of the Gilbert Islands by the U.S. Marines. Tarawa, as the most potentially valuable of the group, would have the highest priority as the focus of an attack. *Dai Honei* reacted vigorously. A fresh garrison and a construction battalion was quickly dispatched from Japan. The Yokosuka Sixth Special Naval Landing Force (1,122 men) arrived on Tarawa on September 15, less than a month after Carlson's raid. The 111th Pioneers (1,247 men) landed in December to begin construction of the island's defenses. Other islands were scoured for Australian and New Zealand coast watchers who, at great personal risk, had performed valiantly by providing intelligence to U.S. headquarters about ship and troop movements. The coast watchers, along with a Protestant missionary and some other white men, were tortured, then killed, thus destroying Allied intelligence in the area, and the garrisons in the Gilberts were increased from fewer than one hundred men to several thousand. By October 6, the Japanese reported that all enemy personnel and communications facilities in the Gilberts had been destroyed.

The Japanese also seized two other islands in the area. On one of them, Nauru, they constructed an airfield garrisoned with 1,400 men; it provided Japanese planes with an increased searching radius of 600 miles. This threat to ships moving between the United States and Australia was greatly magnified by the newly constructed airfield on Betio Island in Tarawa

Atoll that went into service in late January 1943. In February 1943, Rear Adm. Seichiro Tomanari arrived on Betio to take command of the Japanese forces in the Gilbert Islands. On March 17, the Sasebo Seventh Special Naval Landing Force (1,497 men) arrived on Betio. The men of the Special Naval Landing Forces were picked troops sometimes referred to as Imperial Marines; they wore the distinctive anchor and chrysanthemum on their helmets. Finally, in May, the 970 men of the Fourth Fleet Construction Unit arrived on Betio. The construction men, most of whom had some military service, had battle assignments as ammunition handlers, emergency riflemen, or stretcher bearers. The American submarine *Pollack* deprived the Tarawa garrison of another 1,200 men when she sank the *Bankok Maru.*

In August 1943, a year after the Makin raid, Betio Island had been transformed from a sleepy backwater that a hundred men could easily have taken, into a bristling fortress. Since Betio's defenses were nearly complete, their skillful designer, Admiral Tomanari was relieved by the boyish-looking sailor, Adm. Meichi Shibasaki, who would man those defenses against the Second Marine Division. His command was renamed the Third Special Base Force, and given status equal to that of the Kwajalein Base Force in the Marshall Islands.

The New York Times for Friday, August 28, 1942 carried the front page headline "Marines Wiped Out Japanese on Makin Island." Colonel Carlson was quoted as saying that none of the 200 Japanese on Makin were left alive. In fact, the 221 men of Carlson's raiders killed forty-six of the seventy Japanese on Makin, destroyed two planes and a radio station, burned a cache of more than 700 barrels of aviation gasoline, and looted the Japanese commandant's office. The immediate cost was twenty-one marines dead. Nine other marines were left on the island when the Raider Battalion withdrew; they were captured by the Japanese and beheaded. But most of the butcher's bill for the Makin raid came in November 1943 at Betio.

At the Casablanca Conference in January 1943, Roosevelt, Churchill, and the Combined Chiefs of Staff thrashed out the problems of priorities and routes of invasion. One problem was the American insistence on a cross-channel invasion in 1943 for which American forces had been building up in Britain for a year. The British wanted an all-out Mediterranean offensive in 1943 along with increased strategic bombing since their airmen insisted, as airmen always did, that this would destroy German morale and make a cross-channel invasion that much easier. The Americans finally dropped their insistence on a cross-channel invasion in 1943; this released more men for the Pacific since the cross-channel operation was postponed for a year. The Mediterranean invasion so greatly wished for by the British was agreed to. Then Admiral King got his turn to speak.

"Ernie" King was a hard man. Born in Ohio, he was sixty-three in 1943. He had little sense of humor. He was abrupt and often rude. Churchill hated him. U.S. Secretary of War Henry Stimson hated him, as did a number of high British officers. General Dwight Eisenhower, supreme commander in Europe, wrote in his diary: "One thing that might help win this war is to get someone to shoot King. He's the antithesis of cooperation—a deliberately rude person . . . an arbitrary stubborn type, with too much brains and a tendency toward bullying his juniors." King was frequently at daggers drawn with Secretary of the Navy Frank Knox; he got on no better with Undersecretary James Forrestal. The chief of the British General Staff, Gen. Sir Alan Brooke, found King almost unbearable. He was far from loved or even liked in his own branch of the service. But Admiral King had a better strategic grasp of the entire war, both on land and sea, than any other officer in any branch of the Allied service. In addition, at the time of Casablanca, he controlled the limited supply of landing craft that would be needed for invasions anywhere in Europe or Asia; that made him a man whose opinions had to be taken into account however unpleasant his listeners might find it. Even though most of the British delegation were furious with him at one time or another during the conference—and some were furious with him all the time—King got his way in terms of increased support for the Pacific war.

King presented his estimates of the division of forces between the Atlantic and Pacific. He concluded that only 15 percent of the Allies' total war effort was being expended in the Pacific. Admiral King agreed that Germany was the number one target but he argued that if the United States was to retain its initiative against Japan and prevent a new Japanese offensive that might ultimately cause American forces to be withdrawn from Europe the proportion of effort devoted to the Pacific must be at least doubled. As he had written on February 24, 1942 in reply to a query from General Marshall: "The general scheme of things is not only to protect the lines of communications with Australia but . . . to set up 'strong points' from which a general advance can be made through the New Hebrides, Solomons, and the Bismarck Archipelago." Japanese forces in the Pacific were crushing Allied resistance everywhere, but Ernie King—aggressive as always—was talking about "a general advance."

In the final agreement at Casablanca nothing was said about percentages, but there was general understanding that anything not needed for the operation in the Mediterranean would go to the Pacific.

The Casablanca Conference adjourned on February 23, 1943, and Admiral King wasted no time. Even before the conference, on February 9, he had already asked Adm. Chester A. Nimitz for his opinion about seizing the Gilbert and Ellice islands. The commander in chief, Pacific, was unenthusiastic. There were, in his opinion, too few ships and too few trained men to make such an operation feasible.

Further planning by the JCS, however, led by the end of March 1943 to a "Strategic Plan for the Defeat of Japan." This was presented to the "Trident" conference of the Combined Chiefs of Staff in Washington in May and approved by Churchill and Roosevelt.

The JCS conveyed its orders through King or Marshall to Nimitz or MacArthur, respectively. The directives were generally very simple, ordering one or the other to take certain positions by a certain date and outlining what ships, planes, and men would be added to his forces to do that particular job. There was never enough time. Nimitz and his staff could frequently have used a year in which to prepare to do what they had been told to do. Six months would have been barely adequate; they frequently had, as with Guadalcanal, four months or even much less.

The battle over the MacArthur and Nimitz approaches had been refought in April 1943 with the same result. MacArthur wanted everything concentrated on the New Guinea-Mindanao axis. The Joint Chiefs's planners felt that MacArthur's plan would leave the Japanese free to maneuver on the Allied flank, it would not precipitate the decisive naval battle that they were increasingly convinced they could win, and it would allow the Japanese to concentrate their efforts against MacArthur. An American two-pronged approach, however, would divide and confuse the Japanese. The two prongs were finally to fuse to a single spear point at Leyte Gulf. The Joint Chiefs wrote: "There are strong reasons to believe that carrier aircraft, although untested, are equal to the task of supporting amphibious operations against island fortresses in the absence of land-based air." It was an important point because the Army Air Force had been trumpeting to the skies that Midway proved that carriers were no match for land-based aircraft. MacArthur held the same view. In fact, land-based planes, including the Marine fighters from Midway itself, contributed nothing to the mauling of the Japanese fleet. The idea of carrier-supported landings without ground-based support was revolutionary and became the basis for Halsey's thrust northward to the Japanese home islands from Tarawa onward.

By May 20, 1943, however, the Combined Chiefs of Staff had approved the plan for a two-pronged attack by General MacArthur through New Guinea and the Philippines on the west, and by Admiral Halsey through the Gilberts and the Marshalls in the east, with Halsey's attack given preeminence. The problem of command in the South Pacific was a sticky one. Admiral King would never allow the Pacific Fleet to be under MacArthur's control because he was convinced that the general knew nothing about sea power. Similarly, MacArthur would never accept a position subordinate to Nimitz or any other admiral. No one wanted MacArthur brought back to a staff job in Washington. To the Joint Chiefs he posed a threat of becoming the supreme commander whom they had successfully avoided having put over them, and to Roosevelt he was a future political rival.

On July 20 Admiral Nimitz was ordered to invade the Gilbert Islands, and planning began for Operation Galvanic, of which the assault on Tarawa Atoll was the major part. As Admiral King put it: "It appears to me urgent that we take the maximum advantage of this situation (following the Battles of the Coral Sea and Midway) by mounting the operations in the Gilbert-Marshalls at the earliest convenient date practicable, even at the expense of not being completely ready." The JCS plan also removed the Second Marine Division from MacArthur's control for this operation although he retained the First Division.

The Tarawa landing was set for November 15, with the invasion of the Marshall Islands, particularly Kwajalein, to follow a scant six weeks later. The Japanese had built an air base on Kwajalein in the 1930s, and after Pearl Harbor, they built others in the Marshalls on Wotje, Maloelap, Mili (also known as Milli and Mille), and Jaluit. The submarines that had attacked Pearl Harbor had come from Kwajalein as had the assault troops and bombers that subdued Wake Island. The lagoon at Kwajalein was the largest in the world, more than sixty miles long and thirty wide and so remote from Allied airfields that the entire Imperial Combined Fleet could have rendezvoused there undetected.

Speed in taking Tarawa Atoll was essential. Because of the fear of submarine and air attack—the sinking of a loaded transport could cause more casualties than the amphibious landing—and the real possibility of an attack on the invasion force by the Japanese Combined Fleet, only a few days could be allowed for capture of the atoll. As Admiral Spruance wrote in his "General Instructions to Staff Officers, Central Pacific Force, for Galvanic" (in late October 1943): "If a major portion of the Jap Fleet were to attempt to interfere with GALVANIC (The Gilbert Islands operation), it is obvious that the defeat of the enemy fleet would at once become paramount. . . . The destruction of a considerable portion of the Japanese naval strength would . . . go far towards winning the war. . . . We must be prepared at all time during GALVANIC for a fleet engagement."

Preliminary concentration of air or sea bombardment on Betio could not be permitted; it would give the game away. The Second Marine Division under Maj. Gen. Julian Smith was to make the assault, but one-third of the division's infantry forces (the Sixth Marine Regiment) was to be held in Corps reserve. It would not be under Julian Smith's command, but rather under the orders of Gen. Holland M. Smith, who was in turn subordinate to Adm. Richmond Kelly Turner.

Admiral Turner suddenly found himself, on August 24, 1943, in charge of units from both the Army and the Navy departments (including both the Coast Guard and the Marine Corps), ships, planes, and ground forces scattered from New Zealand to Alaska, Hawaii, and California in units most of which he would never see until D-day. Some of the ships were not yet even in commission. "It was (in Adm. Samuel Eliot Morison's words) as if a football coach were required to form a team from different parts of the country, brief them with a manual of plays, and, without even lining them up, send them against a champion opponent." Holland Smith arrived at Pearl Harbor on September 5, 1943, and was told to plan the seizure of the Gilberts.

In late September 1943, *Dai Honei* had a "New Operational Policy" that recognized Japan's changed fortunes since Midway and Guadalcanal. The goal of the new policy was to hold everything then in hand and prepare for a great counteroffensive in the Central and South Pacific in the spring of 1944. Meanwhile, the Imperial Army and Navy were to fight off enemy advances in the southeast (that is, in the Gilberts and Marshalls), wear out and delay the expected Allied offensives in this area and engage the U.S. Fleet in decisive action at an opportune moment, "preferably when tied down to supporting an amphibious operation."

On October 2—a scant six weeks before the invasion of Tarawa Atoll— Gen. Julian Smith heard under what strictures he was being asked to fight. His first angry reaction was to ask to be relieved of command. Stifling that urge, he insisted that it be made clear in his written orders that he had been commanded to make a frontal assault with only a preliminary bombardment and with a third of his forces removed from his command. There was a heavy silence among the commanders gathered around the conference table at Pearl Harbor for a final discussion of *Galvanic,* then "Howling Mad" Smith ("Howling Mad" had been hung on Holland M. Smith when he was a newly commissioned second lieutenant in 1906) barked an order to a subordinate and Gen. Julian Smith got his orders in writing. On October 5 Nimitz issued Operation Plan 13-43 directing the capture and occupation of the Gilberts.

Tarawa's importance lay in the airstrip on Betio. On January 26, 1943, the Liberators of the USAAF, newly stationed at Funafuti, had discovered the airstrip on Betio Island. Use of the Betio airstrip by the U.S. would allow land-based photo-reconnaissance planes to reach Kwajalein in the Marshall Islands, the next targets for Admiral Nimitz's Central Pacific attack. Such an attack was impossible without good photographs of the invasion beaches and their inland defenses, as had been demonstrated in North Africa and again at Guadalcanal. Good photographs meant the use of large, stable platforms for the photographers, in other words, land-based aircraft. No Allied airfield then existed that would allow planes to reach the central Marshalls. It was to seize Betio's airstrip that the marines now assembled as the tropical dawn began to herald a new day over Tarawa Atoll.

3

RED BEACH, RED

Disembarkation was a matter of extreme difficulty for these reasons; the boats drew too much water to be run ashore. . . . The troops . . . with their hands full had at the same time to leap overboard from the boats, stand firm in the water, and fight the enemy.

Julius Caesar: *The Gallic Wars* iv 24.

The red star shell fired from Betio dispelled the idea that no one was left alive on the island, but for some time thereafter there was no further activity ashore. Perhaps the defenders were having the traditional prebattle breakfast of rice, soybean soup, dry chestnuts, and sake. Then, at 0505, the destroyer *Meade* laid a smoke screen to shoreward of *Maryland* to conceal the flash of the ship's catapult as she launched one of her spotting planes. Despite this precaution, the flash was apparently seen, batteries on Betio suddenly opened up, and shells began splashing into the water around *Maryland*. It was clear that workable guns of at least eight-inch bore were being skillfully handled on the island.

Captain Ryan of *Maryland* turned to Admiral Hill, "Shall we go ahead, sir?" The Admiral nodded. Captain Ryan passed the word to the rest of the fire support group on the TBS (Talk Between Ships radio). "Commence firing." Lieutenant Commander Kenneth McArdle tells what happened next:

"Stand by for main battery," came the bark over the ship's p.a. system. Then a warning buzz—a moment later, the after four

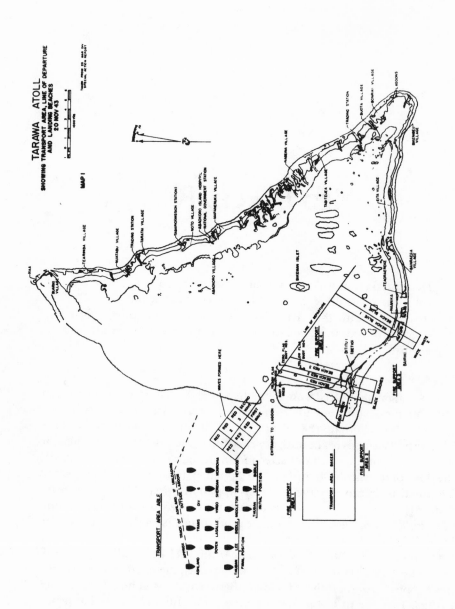

TARAWA ATOLL

SHOWING TRANSPORT AREA, LINE OF DEPARTURE
AND LANDING BEACHES
20 NOV 43

MAP I

sixteen-inchers let go. The big ship flinched as though a giant had struck her with a hammer. Old trouper that she was, she quivered in every corner, and dust filtered down from the overhead fixtures in the combat information center. . . . Then the forward two turrets let go in unison and then they alternated, forward four and after four, wham! wham!

McArdle made two mistakes that morning before *Maryland*'s guns opened up. His first was sleeping through General Quarters, his second was not sleeping in his clothes. He was very nearly trapped below decks as the watertight hatches were closed above him to reduce the ship's vulnerability to being holed and sunk. He got to the bridge only by unscrewing the center panel of a dogged-down hatch and crawling through the twelve-inch opening.

Maryland fired ten salvos of sixteen-inch shells, each as tall as a man and weighing more than a ton. Other guns of the fleet joined in the bombardment, and, as Time-Life correspondent Robert Sherrod later wrote, "The whole island of Betio seemed to erupt with bright fires that were burning everywhere." The bombardment continued until 0542, three minutes before the scheduled air strike from the Southern Carrier Group.

The planes did not appear. There had been a gross misunderstanding. The carrier pilots thought that they were to arrive at sunrise (0612), a more favorable time since they did not then dive out of bright sun onto a target still in darkness. The later time had been agreed to in Hawaii but apparently word had never been passed to Admiral Hill. Aged *Maryland* couldn't hurry the planes along because, when she fired her first sixteen-inch salvo, her radio circuits went out, as they were to do frequently from then on, and they took time to repair. *Maryland* had been modified in Pearl Harbor by having the essential communication center built on. The only place it could go was on a wing of the flag bridge, which was at the same level as the muzzles of the main sixteen-inch battery when the guns were elevated for moderate distance. The renovation was finished by technicians that sailed with *Maryland* from Pearl Harbor to Efate. At Efate single practice shots were fired and there was no trouble with communications, but salvos had not been tried.

The ships of the invasion fleet resumed firing at 0605, but the Japanese gun crews had twenty-three minutes to fire at the transports without fear of being turned into mincemeat by sixteen-inch shells.

There was another foulup as well. Colonel David M. Shoup, who would command the forces ashore and in Betio's lagoon, had asked the Army Air Force to send B-24s to drop 2,000-pound "daisy cutters" along and behind the invasion beaches to kill as many of the defenders as possible. The request was approved by Maj. Gen. Julian Smith, but the planes never appeared and the Army Air Force history of the engagement makes no

INTELLIGENCE MAP BITITU (BETIO) ISLAND
TARAWA ATOLL, GILBERT ISLANDS

SITUATION 1800 D-DAY

.... ADVANCES DURING DAY
ıııııııı POSITIONS AT SUNSET

NOTE: LINES ARE GENERAL INDICATION ONLY.
GAPS WERE COVERED BY SMALL GROUPS
AND BY FIRE. SECONDARY LINES WERE
ESTABLISHED WHERE POSSIBLE BEHIND
FRONT LINES.

TAKEN FROM 2D MAR DIV
SPECIAL ACTION REPORT

500 400 300 200 100 0   1000 YDS

mention of it. There is an unconfirmed story that some of the heavily loaded bombers crashed on take-off and pilots of the other planes refused to fly.

Two transports, *Zeilin* and *Heywood*, were still engaged in the delicate matter of transferring troops into landing craft when they were straddled by Japanese shells and three sailors were hit by shell fragments. The next round would almost certainly have been a catastrophic hit. Three sailors on the other transports had already been wounded by shell fragments, one on *Harris* and two more on *William P. Biddle*. The log of LST-34, which had brought one-third of the precious new amtracs up from Samoa, reads:

> 0612. Enemy shelling from beach by 5″-and 6″-guns commenced. First salvo splashes observed 700 yards off port bow. Second salvo splashes observed 300 yards off port beam.
> 0614. Third salvo 30 yards astern. Underway on evasive courses, speed, forced flank.

Admiral Hill ordered the transports to move out of range; the landing craft had no choice but to go along. The transports finally took station about ten miles offshore. This did not delay the initial assault waves because those men were already in amtracs at the boat rendezvous area south of the transports.

The ships ceased firing again when the bombers from the carriers *Essex, Bunker Hill,* and *Independence* appeared over the island half an hour after Admiral Hill expected them. Seven minutes later the planes had dropped their bombs and gone although they were supposed to have remained over the target for half an hour. The clouds of dust and debris raised by the naval bombardment probably had something to do with the brief time the bombers spent over Betio, and the clouds of confusion over the arrival of the air strike continued to plague its execution. Had the planes arrived when Admiral Hill expected them they would have encountered clear air over Tarawa Atoll.

In any event, the inexperienced pilots of the carrier-based aircraft contributed little that morning to the taking of Betio Island, except for a pilot from the escort carrier *Chenago* who dropped a thousand-pound bomb on the last functioning eight-inch gun ashore, putting both it and its crew out of action forever. But, as Admiral Nimitz later noted, "It was evident that the carrier squadrons were not fully trained to provide efficient air support of amphibious operations."

After the planes departed, the ships began a systematic shelling of every inch of the little island just as Admiral Kingman had promised. The battleships, originally more than six miles offshore, closed in to slightly more than a mile off the west end of the island so that their fire was parallel to the beach on which the landing would be made rather than over the heads of the men in the landing craft. Cruisers followed the battleship's path along the island at twenty- to thirty-minute intervals. The deadly procession then swung eastward and lay-to off the beaches where the marines were scheduled to land. The combined bombardment from three battleships, six cruisers, and nine destroyers lasted two-and-a-half hours. Six million pounds of explosives were hurled onto Betio, or some 1,300 pounds of ordnance for each of the island's defenders. It should have left the island's defenders dead, wounded, or stupefied. It did not.

The torrent of shells poured onto the island with an almost flat trajectory. Like stones skipping across a pond, many of them bounced harmlessly into the ocean beyond. Only plunging fire would have penetrated Betio's cleverly constructed defenses. In addition, the gunners were firing for what is called neutralization rather than destruction. Neutralization fire is shifted rapidly from target to target with emphasis on spraying the enemy landscape with shells in order to hinder organized defense. Destructive fire is slow and deliberate. Most of the shells fired at Betio were not armor piercing. In the early amphibious exercises the targets for naval gunnery had been wooden panels; against those targets armor-piercing shells were worthless, and it became dogma that such ammunition was useless in supporting amphibious operations. In addition, the armor-piercing shells were being kept for use against the Japanese Combined Fleet, should it appear. Some of the big guns on Betio were not destroyed until after the marines were ashore, and those on the eastern end of the island were still firing on the second day of the assault.

Meanwhile, the minesweepers *Pursuit* and *Requisite* swept a channel from the transport area into the lagoon through which the landing craft could pass. At the same time the minesweepers carried on a running duel with the shore batteries. *Pursuit* began sweeping mines out of the pass through the reef shortly after sunrise, her navigation was aided by a Lieutenant Forbes of the Royal New Zealand Navy who was familiar with the waters. The destroyer *Ringgold* entered the lagoon after the mines were swept up; she was also piloted by an officer of the Royal New Zealand Navy, Lt. Gordon J. Webster. After the sweep, *Pursuit* split off to follow Lt. Comdr. Robert A. MacPherson, flying one of *Maryland*'s Kingfisher float planes, as he guided the vessel to shoals (easily visible from the air), which *Pursuit*'s crew then marked with smoke pots. As is usual in tropical waters the lagoon was studded with coral heads and reefs that made navigation hazardous except when good light was available (for some few hours before and a few hours after noon).

Maryland's other plane, with Lt. (jg.) F. C. Whaley at the controls, was used to observe the effects of the naval bombardment on the tiny island.

Ringgold took a shell in the port engine room and another passed through the sick bay and the emergency radio room. But *Ringgold* was a lucky ship; both shells failed to explode, although the shell in the engine room shut off water, steam, and electricity to the after part of the vessel. *Ringgold* then trained her own guns on the battery tormenting her. A salvo from *Ringgold* hit the shore battery's ammunition dump, and the gun emplacement and its crew disappeared in a towering column of smoke and flame.

All four ships now began to fire directly into the beach defenses behind the objectives of the first three waves of landing craft that were splashing clumsily toward the beach. The minesweeper *Pursuit* also stationed herself to mark the line of departure at which the landing craft would make a turn to starboard (right) and head directly into the beach. The *Pursuit*'s searchlight served the little vessels as a beacon through the dust and smoke of the lagoon. Busy with firing at the shore batteries, *Pursuit* stationed herself farther north than she should have. This meant a longer trip to the beach for the first three waves than had been planned for.

One disadvantage of the attack on the northern beaches was the long run for the landing craft. After forming into waves in the area between the transports and the pass into the lagoon, the vessels had three-and-a-half miles to go before reaching the line of departure in the lagoon and another three miles from there to the beach.

H-hour, the time at which the first waves of amtracs were to hit the beaches assigned to them, was 0830. By then, some of the marines, sailors, and coastguardsmen had been pitching about in the little craft for nearly five hours. They were willing to fight anyone just to get away from the landing craft and their gut-emptying motion.

After loading troops, the Marine drivers of the amtracs and the Navy coxswains of the Higgins boats had lined up their vessels in the designated rendezvous area. From there, the amtracs of the first three waves had departed at 0645 for the line of departure three-and-a-half miles away. The craft could make four-and-a-half knots in calm water; they were expected to arrive on that line in one hour or less after leaving the rendezvous.

They did not. Outside the lagoon there was a strong westerly current and choppy seas; the amtrac's average speed was slightly less than four knots, the pace of a brisk walk. Besides the effects of the current, the older amtracs that made up the bulk of the forces were not performing as well as they had earlier. The amtracs in the first wave were those brought from New Zealand since it was certain that they would be on hand on D-day (the arrival of the new amtracs via LST from Samoa had been less certain). Thus, the first wave was made up of the older and slower amtracs.

At twelve minutes before eight, Lieutenant Commander MacPherson reported from his plane that the amtracs were still half a mile from the line of departure. Admiral Hill's teeth clenched on his pipe stem; he had no choice but to postpone H-hour for an additional fifteen minutes. Shortly after that it was moved up again, to 0900. The first wave of amtracs crossed the line of departure, some 6,000 yards from the beach, at 0824. The Hellcat fighters from the escort carriers began strafing the beaches at 0830, and the gunfire support ships were ordered to resume firing for fifteen minutes beginning at 0840.

Even these postponements were not enough. The first wave arrived at the beach at 0910. There was no further support fire from outside the lagoon because there was a dense cloud of smoke over much of the island. Admiral Hill feared that shells might fall amidst the landing craft. Thus the Japanese defenders, who could tell from the approach of the amtracs where the blows would fall, had nearly twenty minutes to transfer men to defend the northern beaches and to fire on the landing craft as they wallowed toward the shore. The strafing planes were a nuisance, but the Japanese moved in covered trenches where possible, and the .50-caliber slugs from the planes bounced harmlessly off the prepared gun emplacements on the northern beaches.

The carrier pilots, although they were supposed to begin strafing when the amtracs were only a few hundred yards from the beach, began instead when the tractors were still two and a quarter miles out. The planes stopped strafing when the vessels were only halfway to the beach from the line of departure. The effect of the strafing, modest at best, was largely dissipated by the time the first amtrac slithered up onto the narrow beach some fifteen minutes later.

Admiral Turner's order read: "Time of strafing beaches with references to H-hour is approximate. The distance of the boats from the beach is the governing factor. When the first wave of boats has approached to 1000 yards from Red Beaches strafe installations from the water's edge to 100 yards inland."

The men in the landing craft had plenty of time to take cautious looks at the island and to attempt to square what they saw with the information they had been given about Betio and its defenses. On November 14, signal lights from the flagship winked out Admiral Hill's message to the transports:

> Give all hands the general picture of the projected operation and further details to all who should have this in execution of duties. This is the first American assault on a strongly defended atoll and, with northern (Makin) attack and covering forces, the largest Pacific operation to date.

Marine Gunnery Sergeant Hank Gregerson had bet a lot of money that the target would be Betio because of a tip a buddy had given him back in New Zealand. After the word was out he went to collect, but without success. Payday was late, and Sergeant Gregerson was worried. He would not be paid until after the invasion and some of the men who owed him money might be dead. But there was nothing he could do.

The information given the men after Admiral Hill's message was massive in amount, precise in detail, and almost supernaturally accurate. Once the target for Operation Galvanic was selected, intelligence officers of the Army, Navy, and Marine Corps swung into action. They pored over old maps, charts, and accounts of life on Tarawa. They interviewed people who had lived on the atoll and they asked for all the up-to-date reconnaissance information they could get.

In fact, in January 1943, two weeks before Admiral King had first sounded out Admiral Nimitz on the Gilbert Islands operation, three B-24 Liberators of the Seventh Army Air Force made a combined bombing and photographic reconnaissance run over Tarawa. It was then that the airstrip on Betio was discovered. On September 18 and 19, a little more than two months before the invasion, carrier planes from Rear Admiral Pownell's Fast Carrier Force (TF50), including *Lexington, Princeton,* and *Belleau Wood* made seven strikes on Tarawa, destroying half of the planes at the airfield and killing and wounding some of the defenders. As a Japanese artilleryman in the Sixth Yokosuka Special Naval Landing Force wrote in his diary: "The island is a sea of flames. Seven of our medium attack bombers were destroyed and a great number of our guns were damaged. Moreover, shell dumps, ammunition dumps, various storehouses and barracks on Bairiki (the island just east of Betio) were destroyed. A great number of men were killed or wounded."

Another result of this bombing was that Admiral Shibasaki ordered the immediate construction of a bombproof communications center; it was to be completed in October. This facility was to cause the marines considerable difficulty. In early September there had been eighteen planes on the island and 330 air support personnel. After the U.S. bombing later that month, most of the air units were evacuated, and Tarawa was never again used as a Japanese air base.

A most important result of these raids was that *Lexington's* planes took a set of low oblique photos of the lagoon side of Betio.

Because of the great distances involved (round trips of over 2,400 miles for the B-24Ds) and the small size of the targets, pinpoint navigation was required. Planes commonly failed to find their targets. In the September 18th raid that did so much damage, only eighteen of two dozen B-24s reached the target. There were other hazards as well. On the 19th the carrier planes were followed by twenty B-24s. Antiaircraft fire and a force of fifteen to twenty Zeros shot down one B-24 and damaged ten others.

As D-day approached the pace of bombing raids increased, both against Tarawa and the Japanese airfields that could launch planes against the invasion fleet. The B-24s hit Tarawa on D-6 (six days before the landing began), D-3, and D-1, the last time in coordination with carrier aircraft. Mili was also bombed on D-6 and again the next day when Jaluit was also hit. Kwajalein and Maloelap were bombed on D-4 and Mili again on D-3.

The bombers encountered antiaircraft fire of various degrees of intensity and accuracy over all the targets and enemy aircraft over Kwajalein, Jaluit, and Maloelap. Enemy planes struck back at the American airfields at Funafuti and Nanomea several times as D-day approached. These actions cost the Seventh Bombing Group (of the Seventh Air Force, although under operational control of the Navy) five planes and thirty-six casualties. The B-24Ds were sadly lacking in firepower, especially forward, and the Japanese pilots soon learned to attack frontally. Throughout 1943 the B-24s were modified to remedy these defects, in part through a nose turret.

The carrier plane raid on September 19 cost the Navy two Dauntless dive-bombers, one Hellcat fighter, and one Avenger torpedo bomber lost to antiaircraft fire.

A Fleet Air Photographic Squadron photographed the island on October 20 and again some three weeks later. At the time of the first flight of the Navy photo planes, an Army reconnaissance plane also photographed the island from 20,000 feet.

To add to the misery of Betio's defenders, the island was bombarded by three U.S. cruisers on D-1 for a little more than two hours. They fired nearly 2,000 eight-inch shells and eighty-two five-inch shells.

Some of the marines heading for Betio might have held little respect for the men who developed photographs in darkrooms and the intelligence analysts bent over maps and papers piled on cluttered desks. Still, the work of these groups, like that of the legion of civilian and military workers who tediously calculated what supplies and in what quantities would be needed at Tarawa Atoll and then arranged to get them there, was essential to the success of the military action. It was as important to the outcome as the skill, strength, and courage of the combat infantry that actually fought the battle.

There is an apocryphal story, attributed by some writers to Colonel Shoup and by a Marine captain to himself, of how the number of Japanese troops on Betio was determined by examination of aerial photographs of the number of privies on the island. However, Marine Maj. Thornton Hinkle of the Navy's Combat Intelligence Unit apparently determined the number of troops on Tarawa Atoll in the usual order-of-battle way. Since he knew that the Sasebo Seventh Special Naval Landing Force, the Sixth Special Naval Landing Force, the 111th Pioneers, and a Fourth Fleet Construction Unit were on the island, he could calculate fairly closely how many men were there. He was within 100 of the final total.

Another extremely useful photographic mission, in addition to the aerial reconnaissance, was that of the submarine *Nautilus* whose periscope was fitted with a camera bracket. The Navy had supplied three cameras presumably purchased, as usual, from the lowest bidder. None worked. Fortunately, the ship's executive officer, Lt. Comdr. R. B. Lynch, was a camera enthusiast and his German-made Leica saved the day. It was one of many contributions of the Axis powers to their own defeat. Beginning on September 25, *Nautilus* spent eighteen days making a thorough reconnaissance in the Gilberts and obtaining a continuous water level panorama (over 2,000 photographs) of the coastlines. Since it was late October before she returned to Pearl Harbor, the intelligence officers, mostly of Nimitz's Joint Intelligence Center, Pacific Ocean Areas, at Pearl Harbor, worked day and night to put all this and other information together into a composite picture of Betio and its environs.

As the convoy sailed toward Betio, the men had access to a huge model of the island on which one inch equaled 250 feet. They could see from the model and the maps that Tarawa Atoll is triangular; its eastern and southern legs, thirteen and twelve miles long, respectively, are composed of long narrow islands on which grow coconut palms. The western leg of the triangle is all barrier reef except for two deep-water passes into the lagoon.

They were also told that tiny Betio bristled with gun barrels as a porcupine bristles with quills. There were four British-built eight-inch Vickers guns that the Japanese had captured at Singapore. These guns were mounted at both ends of the island from where they could sweep the north beach where the marines would land.

The Japanese also had ten smaller coast-defense guns, a dozen antiaircraft guns that could also be used against surface targets, and nearly a hundred other emplaced weapons ranging from the vicious 7.7-mm (0.3-inch) machine guns through 75-mm (3-inch) battalion and mountain guns. The defenses of Betio also included double-apron high-wire fences on the reef near the beach and similar low-wire fences on the beach itself together with concrete tetrahedrons to channel approaching boats into lanes swept by the antiboat guns. The American intelligence officers knew nothing of the 7.7-mm Type 92 Nambu machine guns, and they missed more than a third of the other weapons that were smaller than the coast-defense guns.

This was not negligence. The big weapons had to be mounted in the open. Many of the smaller guns were inside well-concealed log, steel, or reinforced concrete emplacements covered with sand; these did not show up on aerial photographs. There were forty-four such positions for the 7.7-mm machine guns, and sixty-two for 13-mm (0.5-inch) machine guns. Admiral Shibasaki had had most of the fourteen light tanks that had come to Betio with the Sasebo force dug into pits and their 37-mm (1.5-inch) gun barrels camouflaged with palm fronds. As the marines were to learn, this was one of the most effective ways to use light tanks.

The marines also knew that this was a new kind of operation—one that had been considered impossible since the fiasco at Gallipoli in 1915—an assault from the sea against a heavily fortified beach. As Lord Nelson had put it (with dubious syntax but unmistakable meaning), "A ship's a fool to fight a fort." What chance, then, had mere men, no matter how brave? The previous major invasions in which the marines had participated were on large islands. Guadalcanal was ninety miles long and twenty-five miles wide. Bougainville was even wider and half again as long. On such large land masses the Japanese defenders had not heavily fortified every beach where an invasion force might land, although they did fortify some of the more obvious spots to harass invading troops. The main defensive forces, however, were kept inland until the invasion point was established, then they were sent in to pinch it off.

Tiny Betio was different. Few points on the island were more than 300 yards (about two average city blocks) from water, so that nearly all the defensive weapons could be brought to bear on forces approaching the island from any direction. And defensive weapons were superabundant. Nor was this the end of the island's defenses. The Japanese had carefully used their time on Betio. Besides the mined concrete boat obstacles, there were cairns built of coral, and barbed wire and log barricades to channel landing craft into lanes that practically led them down the barrels of shore-based artillery. Along the perimeter of the island, a few feet behind the beach, there was a wall three feet high, made largely of coconut logs wired and stapled together. At high water there was no beach, the waves broke directly against the log wall. Behind the wall was a network of machine-gun emplacements. There were also the covered fortifications described above, connected by a network of trenches and containing rifle ports, command posts, and ammunition dumps.

Fortunately for the marines, the defenses at the western and northern beaches remained incomplete because, after November 18, Admiral Shibasaki's men had to work incessantly to repair damage from the frequent air raids, and they were hindered by a shortage of cement due to interrupted shipping. Admiral Shibasaki had requested 690,000 more tons of cement, enough men to build twenty-three additional artillery emplacements, and the weapons to fill them.

Bombproof shelters were placed about the island and were so constructed that they were immune to anything but direct hits from the largest guns, and even then only if armor-piercing shells or other delayed action projectiles were used. As we have seen, Task Force 53 would not expend many armor-piercing shells on Betio because they had to conserve them to meet the very real threat of a naval battle with the powerful Combined Imperial Fleet.

There were also the island's natural defenses. Besides the suffocating heat there were extensive coral reefs surrounding the island, and over these swirled the unpredictable tides of Tarawa. As the official Army historians later concluded, "Tarawa was the most heavily defended atoll that would ever be invaded by Allied forces in the Pacific. With the possible exception of Iwo Jima, its beaches were better protected against a landing force than any encountered in any theater of war throughout World War II."

Admiral Shibasaki had declared that the Americans could not take Tarawa with a million men. The commander of the First Japanese Combat Unit on Betio had issued an order:

> . . . to defend to the last man all vital areas and destroy the enemy at the water's edge. In a battle where the enemy is superior, it is necessary to lure him within range of our fixed defense installations, and then, using all our strength, destroy him.

They nearly succeeded.

Betio was best described by correspondent Robert Sherrod who compared its shape to that of a bird (see the Tarawa Atoll map). The tufted head of the Betio bird is at the western end of the island, its beak makes the northwestern point, while its tail is the eastern tip. From head to tail it is two and a quarter miles long and less than a half mile wide at its widest place. The Betio bird lies on its left side; its legs are formed by the long pier that juts out 500 yards into the lagoon to the edge of the reef from the northern beach on which the marines were to land. At the seaward end of the pier there was a Y-shaped seaplane ramp. Beach Red 1 was the throat of the Betio bird and ran southeast to the underside of the beak. Beach Red 2 extended from just east of the main pier to Red 1. The most easterly beach, Beach Red 3, joined Red 2 in the west, then ran eastward to a point almost directly north of the end of the Japanese airfield. The beaches were 500 to 800 yards long or a bit less than a half mile each.

It was clear from the reconnaissance pictures that the defenders of Betio expected attack on either the south or the west beaches. There defenses were heaviest, so also was the surf. For these and other reasons these beaches were unattractive to the invasion planners. The northeastern beaches offered less room to maneuver for the landing forces once ashore, they were also heavily defended, and they could be swept by flanking fire from the remainder of the island. The northwestern beaches, though not without disadvantages for the attacking marines, were finally chosen.

The Third Battalion, Second Regiment, Second Marine Division was known in Corps jargon as the Third Battalion, Second Marines or, more simply still, as 3/2. It was commanded by Maj. John F. Schoettel and, for Operation Galvanic, was designated as Landing Team One (LT 1). It arrived off Tarawa aboard the transport *Heywood* and its objective was Beach Red 1. Lieutenant Colonel Herbert R. Amey commanded the Second Battalion, Second Marines (2/2, or Landing Team Two). They were to sail from the transport *Zeilin* to Beach Red 2. Beach Red 3 was the goal of Maj. Henry Pierson Crowe, whose Second Battalion, Eighth Marine Regiment (2/8, or LT3) had come from Wellington, New Zealand, in *Arthur Middleton*. Major Crowe was a big, burly, red-bearded, former All-Marine football star. He sported a bushy red moustache that curled jauntily upwards at the ends. His executive officer was a striking contrast to Major Crowe, who was a former enlisted man who had worked his way up through Marine ranks. Major William C. Chamberlin was short, blond, and bespectacled. He was a Phi Beta Kappa and had been a professor of economics at Northwestern University when the war began.

Each of the first three assault waves carried elements of all three landing teams. The forty-two old amtracs of the first wave (followed by five empty amtracs as spares) were to land at H-hour, the second and third waves in the new amtracs (also with five spares) were to land at three-minute intervals thereafter. There were fifteen to twenty-five marines in each amtrac, in all some 1,500 men made up the first three waves. The defenders of Betio, after being subjected to air and sea bombardment and now watching the long lines of amtracs wallowing toward the shore, must have been reminded of the legendary Japanese demon *Hiru-Daikokuten* that had three heads and six arms.

The first wave of amtracs ground ashore at Beach Red 1 ahead of the boats destined for the other beaches, although Major Schoettel's men had further to go. They arrived at ten minutes after H-hour, or 0910; the second and third waves landed at two-minute intervals after that. On Beaches Red 2 and Red 3 the first waves arrived simultaneously with the second and third waves, but not until 0922. But a simple recounting of time and place cannot describe the confusion, terror, and death that washed over the men of the first three waves after 0830 Saturday, November 20, 1943.

Navy and Marine observers alike were convinced that the bombardment of Betio had devastated the defenders. They were soon disillusioned. One fire-control officer who landed early was "quite unnerved upon closer approach to the beach to see many batteries of all calibers still firing at the waves engaged in landing." About 700 yards out from the beach the tractors came under machine-gun fire but none of them were stopped. About 200 yards out they were fired on by all types of weapons and were severely mauled. Soon they were close enough to distinguish the characteristic whine of the long Ariska rifles used by the Japanese. The amtracs that successfully reached the beach were careful to back off before turning around because they were not armored astern.

Landing Team One under Major Schoettel, a prematurely bald, athletic-looking man from Lima, Ohio, with a degree in pharmacy from the University of Washington, was the first to reach shore. They sailed into a terrifying situation. The reef apron is wide on Beach Red 1 and the amtracs risked close-range fire from both ahead and to the right as they sailed in. The well-disciplined Japanese troops held their fire until the landing craft were within 100 yards of shore. There is an ancient Japanese boyhood game of courage called *shibedate*, standing a rice stalk on end. The first boy would place an object on a grave, the second would retrieve it. The third boy would stick a rice stalk on the grave, and the cycle would begin again until someone lost his nerve. The boys believed that fear came only if their scrotums shrank, so, as they walked toward the grave, they would pluck at them to keep them stretched. There may have been many stretched scrotums among the defenders of Betio as the amtracs drove up on the reef, but the Japanese restrained themselves until the last moment.

Then rifles, light and heavy machine guns, antiboat guns, and coast-defense guns let go in a shrieking nightmare of sound, killing the drivers of the amtracs, disabling the vessel's engines, and igniting their fuel. Samuel Eliot Morison quoted Pvt. N. M. Baird, an Oneida Indian who wrote:

Bullets pinged off that tractor like hailstones off a tin roof. Two shells hit the water twenty yards off the port (left) side and sent up regular geysers. I swept the beach (with one of the two machine guns the amtracs carried) just to keep the bastards down as much as possible. Can't figure out how I didn't get it in the head or something.

We were 100 yards in now and the enemy fire was awful damn intense and gettin' worse. They were knockin' boats out right and left. A tractor'd get hit, stop, and burst into flames, with men jumping out like torches. . . . Bullets ricocheted off the coral and up under the tractor. It must've been one of those bullets that got the driver. The boat lurched and I looked in the cab and saw him slumped over. The lieutenant jumped in and pulled the driver out, and drove himself until he got hit.

That happened about thirty yards off shore. A shell struck the boat. The concussion felt like a big fist—Joe Louis maybe—had smacked me right in the face. Seemed to make my face swell up. Knocked me down and sort of stunned me for a moment. . . . My assistant, a private with a Mexican name, was feeding my gun, had his pack and helmet blown right off. He was crumpled up beside me, with his head forward, and in the back of it was a hole I could put my fist in. I started to shake him and he fell right on over.

Guys were sprawled all over the place. I looked across at my buddy, who was only five feet from me. He was on his back and his face was all bloody and he was holding his hand over his face and mumbling something.

Our boat was stopped and they were laying lead to us like holy hell. Everybody seemed to be stunned, so I yelled, "Let's get the hell out of here."

I grabbed my carbine and an ammunition box and stepped over a couple of fellas lying there and put my head up. The bullets were pouring at us like a sheet of rain. . . . Only about a dozen out of the twenty-five went over the side with me and only about four of us ever got evacuated.

Companies I and K of Major Schoettel's battalion got ashore without serious losses but Company K landed close to a Japanese strong point at the junction of Red Beach 1 and 2 and instantly took heavy casualties. Company I was farther away from the strong point and somewhat protected in the early minutes after reaching the beach. But both companies suffered fifty percent casualties in the first two hours. The remaining company (L), under the command of Maj. Michael Ryan, waded ashore from 500 yards out. Gunnery Sergeant Hank Gregerson was in L Company. Worrying about collecting on his bets on the Second Division's destination occupied his mind for a while on the way to the beach, but when his amtrac was disabled he suddenly had more pressing matters to think about. He need not have worried about the bets. Sergeant Gregerson died in the water off Red Beach 1. His company lost 35 percent of its men before they reached the beach on the western end of the island.

It was slightly better elsewhere. Landing Team Two reached Beach Red 2 without experiencing the horrors that befell LT 1, but the commanding officer, Lt. Col. Herbert Amey, a tall, handsome, black-haired man with a black moustache, was caught in a burst of machine-gun fire and killed while wading ashore after the amtrac to which he had transferred from a Higgins boat was stopped by the barbed wire off the beach. When he told his men of their assignment he had said:

> We are very fortunate. This is the first time a landing has been made by American troops against a well-defended beach, the first time over a coral reef, the first time against any force to speak of, and the first time the Japs have had the hell kicked out of them in a hurry.

When he finished his speech the shy colonel was dripping with perspiration. Now he was dead without ever setting foot on the dry sand of Betio Island.

Lieutenant Colonel Amey's executive officer, Maj. Howard J. Rice, landed out of position, so most of the battalion found themselves on the beach at Betio without their top commanders. An observer from the Fourth Marine Division, Lt. Col. Walter I. Jordan, assumed command. Because the defenders were still somewhat disorganized, most of LT 2 got to the beach, but once there they were subjected to such merciless fire that most of the men could only cringe behind the log barrier where they were comparatively safe.

The amtrac drivers of the boats carrying Major Crowe's Landing Team Three found two-thirds of the beach so cluttered with coral blocks that all seventeen of the amtracs landed on the western portion of Beach Red 3. This area was still comparatively lightly defended, in part because the two destroyers in the lagoon continued firing on that portion of the beach for twenty-one minutes after other naval gunfire had stopped. Two amtrac drivers even found a break in the beach barrier and discharged their troops about 100 yards inland. It was only a temporary triumph. Not surprisingly, these marines soon found themselves in danger of being outflanked and had to withdraw to a stronger position.

Of the 522 men of the Second Battalion, Eighth Marines who started for Red Beach 3, fewer than twenty-five were killed or wounded before they reached the beach. Of the six commissioned and noncommissioned officers in Company E, however, five were killed or wounded as they hit the beach. Casualties among commissioned and noncommissioned officers were extremely high throughout the battle for Betio Island. Only commissioned and noncommissioned officers in the Marine Corps wear the blood red stripes on their dress blue trousers because it was they who did most of the bleeding at Chapultepec in 1847 on the way to the halls of Montezuma. It was the same at Tarawa Atoll.

In the first three waves (some ninety amtracs in all), at least eight of the tractors did not make the beach, and most of the .50-caliber machine gunners were killed. Some fifteen more of the amtracs sank when they again reached deep water. This is the more significant because the defenders of Betio, stunned by the prolonged bombardment, had not fully manned the island's defenses until the first three waves were already ashore. Before the battle was over four of every five members of the amtrac crews were dead or wounded including the amtrac battalion commander, Maj. Henry Drewes, who died that first day with a bullet through his brain.

The Marines' light tanks, not very useful weapons in the best of circumstances, had a hard time as well. Three of the four tanks of the Second Platoon, Second Tank Battalion reached Beach Red 3 and moved west to Beach Red 2. Moving inland, one tank dropped into a shell hole and one was destroyed, probably by a mine. The Third Platoon got all four of its light tanks ashore on Beach Red 3. These were ordered to move inland, but one was destroyed by a friendly dive-bomber, two others were put out of action by enemy gunfire. The other was set on fire but was salvaged and remained in action.

Most of the fourth wave was made up of sea-blue Higgins boats (LCVPs) loaded with 37-mm guns that were badly needed ashore. Because of the low tide, however, many of these boats could not reach the beach until nightfall. The three battalion commanders of the assault troops on the beach were also in the fourth wave. Only one battalion commander, Major Crowe, got ashore alive and in the proper position to command his men. In most cases, the commissioned officers, the NCOs, and the men they led were strangers; that made the exercise of command difficult. It was thirty-six hours after the initial landing before a fully organized Marine unit existed on Betio.

Private, first class Donald Libby had a spectacular experience that stood out even on Betio where such experiences were almost commonplace. He was hit in both thighs by bullets as his amtrac approached the beach. Then the amtrac was hit by a shell that killed almost everyone on board. The explosion of the shell hurled him out of the amtrac and into the water bleeding profusely from the bullet wounds in his thighs and seven shrapnel wounds. He spotted a life preserver and hung onto it for several hours. Then, as the tide was carrying him out to sea someone waded out to him wearing a Marine helmet and carrying a bayonet.

"What state are you from?" said the wading man.

"Maine," Libby answered, and found that he could stand up in the water. "And where are you from?"

The wader's home was somewhere in Japan, as he proved by lunging at Libby with his bayonet. Libby tried to ward off the blow with his left hand. The bayonet went through it. Libby then grabbed the bayonet with his right hand, wrenched it away from the Japanese, and swung at him with the hilt. He hit his assailant behind the ear, then hit him again on the forehead as he fell into the water. After that, Libby held the man's head under water until he drowned. Hours later another amtrac found Libby, wrinkled as a prune, still bleeding, but alive, and Pfc. Donald Libby's battle was over.

The fifth wave of landing craft was made up of LCMs (Landing Craft, Mechanized) loaded with Sherman medium tanks, also vitally needed to deal with the strong Japanese emplacements. The LCMs discharged the tanks in three or four feet of water after Major Schoettel turned back two of them that were withdrawing from Red Beach 1. The six thirty-ton Shermans then moved slowly toward the shore preceded by a Marine guide who led them around the many potholes, some seven feet deep, in the coral. Most of the guides were killed or wounded before the tanks were ashore. The holes were only one type of obstacle. When they reached the beach they found it covered with the bodies of dead and wounded marines. The tank commander then chose to lead his tanks around the beak of the Betio bird to Green Beach. The tanks swerved continually to avoid potholes, but visibility is poor from inside a tank. Sometimes wounded men were crushed under the tank treads, at other times the tank veered into a pothole while trying to avoid marine bodies. Four of the six tanks sank into potholes and drowned out their engines. The other two got ashore on Green Beach. One was later hit and burned, the other was disabled.

All the medium tanks came from C Company, Corps Tank Battalion (for this reason all the tanks' names started with C). They were loaded into lighters (LCMs) aboard the LST *Ashland*, the hold was then flooded and the lighters floated out on their own. When they were unloaded from the LCMs they were about 800 yards offshore and the water came nearly to their turrets.

Three tanks of the Second Tank Platoon got ashore on Red Beach 2, one dropped into a shell hole and couldn't be extricated, another was blown up. The Third Platoon got ashore on Red Beach 3 without losing a tank. Then one was knocked out by a friendly dive-bomber, and two others were disabled by enemy fire. By the end of D-day, of the twelve Shermans (three platoons) that had been debarked by the LCMs at the reef only two were still in action.

Despite these difficulties, more than half of the medium tanks unloaded (nine of fourteen) reached Betio Beach around noon on D-day, although on the heavily defended Beach Red 1, of six tanks that started for it only two got to the beach.

Reaching shore was only part of the problem. Like the drivers of the new amtracs, the tank crews had not trained with the battalion landing teams, and communication between the riflemen and the tank crews was poor. The marines had never had Sherman tanks before. As the tank battalion commander, Lt. Col. Alexander Swenceski later recalled: "We did not lose a man inside the tanks, but most of them were lost getting out and trying to communicate with the infantry."

On D-day, Lieutenant Colonel Swenceski had to abandon his tank in shallow water when it was disabled by enemy fire; he himself was seriously wounded. In his last lucid moments, he realized that he could not reach the beach and that if he collapsed on the coral, as had so many other wounded marines, he would drown at high tide. Swenceski dragged himself painfully to the top of a pile of dead marines and lay there, as if dead himself, throughout the rest of D-day, the following night, and well into the next day.

Colonel David Monroe Shoup commanded the Second Regiment, Second Marine Division, and ended up leading all forces ashore on Betio as well as those in the lagoon. Colonel Shoup, a farm boy from Indiana and a marine since 1926, was a short, broad, red-faced, and bull-necked man of thirty-nine whose grammar belied the fact that he had been an A student at DePauw University with a major in mathematics. Most important, he was a tough and able Marine officer.

Colonel Shoup was initially in an LCVP (Higgins boat) and in radio contact with his battalion commanders. The Higgins boat couldn't reach the beach so Shoup hailed an amtrac outbound with wounded men. Most of the wounded had, in fact, already died, and Shoup ordered the amtrac driver to help throw the bodies into the water, then the amtrac headed back toward the beach carrying Shoup; Lt. Col. E. Carlson of Raider fame; Maj. T. Culhane; Lt. Col. P. Rixey (artillery commander, First Battalion, Tenth Marines); Commander Nelson, the regimental surgeon; and a sergeant with a radio. They headed originally for the left half of Red Beach 2, but the fire was so heavy that they withdrew to the end of the pier and joined a line of LCMs carrying tanks toward Red Beach 3. One hundred yards from shore two 77-mm guns opened up sinking one LCM instantly and causing another to sink slowly. Shoup's amtrac went back to the end of the pier to try Red Beach 2 again, but the engine went out and the passengers had to jump over the side. Colonel Shoup reached the long pier about 1100 and directed the battle as best he could while standing alongside the pier in waist-deep water made cloudy with pulverized coral and thick with the silvery bodies of fish killed by concussion.

The situation ashore was about as bad as it could be. The reef extending from Beaches Red 2 and 3 was swept by cross-fire from three directions. At least twenty amtracs and two LCMs, full of dead and wounded men, were impaled on the reef. One Japanese gun crew on the tail of the Betio bird was spectacularly accurate. Several times, just as the ramp of a Higgins boat splashed down so the troops could leap into the water and begin wading ashore, the gun dropped a shell right onto the landing craft, spreading a pool of blood around the wreckage. The gun was finally silenced by fire from the destroyers in the lagoon.

One Higgins-boat coxswain panicked and let down the ramp while he was still seaward of the reef. He screamed, "This is as far as I go." The marines, unaware of how far out they were, jumped out into fifteen feet of water. Many drowned.

Even before Colonel Shoup reached the long pier he had begun to worry about Major Schoettel's men on Beach Red 1. Just before 1000, Shoup received a message from Schoettel who was still afloat in the fourth wave. It read, "Receiving heavy fire all along beach. Unable to land all. Issue in doubt." A later message told of the inability of boats to land on the right flank of Beach Red 1. Shoup then advised Schoettel to land on Beach Red 2 and work west. To this message, Schoettel sent a lugubrious reply. "We have nothing left to land."

At 1103 Major Crowe's Third Battalion, Eighth Marines (3/8), under command of Maj. Robert H. Ruud, were ordered ashore on Beach Red 3 to reinforce their comrades (2/8) already on the beach. The moment their Higgins boats grounded on the reef the coxswains lowered the ramps, and the marines rushed out to begin wading ashore. Unfortunately, the boats had grounded amidships; the water at the bows was often more than six feet deep, and again, many of the equipment-laden marines drowned. Mortar, 40-mm (1.6-inch) cannon, and machine-gun fire further disorganized the formation and caused heavy casualties.

Lieutenant Commander Robert MacPherson, watching the battle below from his observation plane, wrote in his log: "The water never seemed clear of tiny men, their rifles over their heads, slowly wading beachward. I wanted to cry." MacPherson may have seemed safely above the battle, but he wasn't. When he landed alongside Maryland later that afternoon, his rear-seat gunner was wounded and there was a line of bullet holes in the aircraft's fuselage. MacPherson was a methodical man. He had spent the evening before the assault tidying up his gear so that it would be easy to send home if he didn't come back from his hazardous missions.

By noon, Colonel Shoup had gotten ashore.

The Associated Press correspondent William Hipple reported:

> A big shell came so close that the concussion knocked him over in the water and badly wrenched one of his knees. Up in a moment, he refused an offer of help and told all to go forward. Colonel Shoup crawled into the hole I was occupying with the other men and said, "Okay, let's get going. If we don't secure a piece of this island by nightfall we're in a spot." He immediately established a command post behind a Jap air raid shelter.

David Shoup and his young runner waded ashore hand in hand. Just as they reached the beach a bullet hit the young man and killed him; Colonel Shoup himself was lacerated by shell fragments that tore into his legs.

By then some 1,500 marines were pinned down on the beach against the barrier wall. Replacements, bigger guns, water, medical supplies, and ammunition could not come ashore because of the low tide and the shortage of available amtracs. The marines, confronted with guns emplaced in pillboxes, couldn't advance. Their training in cooperative attack against such obstacles had been sadly deficient.

In New York City that Saturday night, the curtain was going up on Katherine Cornell and Raymond Massey in the frothy comedy *Friends and Lovers,* on Ethyl Barrymore in *The Corn Is Green,* on Paul Robeson in *Othello,* and on those hardy perennials *Tobacco Road* and *Life with Father.* There was also the new musical *Oklahoma.* At the movies there were Ingrid Bergman and Gary Cooper in *For Whom the Bell Tolls,* Ingrid Bergman and Humphrey Bogart in *Casablanca,* and Greer Garson in *Mrs. Miniver.* These offered housewives momentary relief from the problems of trying to feed and clothe their families when the butter, meat, and hard cheese ration was only two pounds a week and the shoe ration three pairs per year. Canned foods were rationed because tin went into armaments and C-ration cans, coffee because the ships to carry it from South America had been requisitioned for military purposes, shoes because the Army needed some fifteen million pairs of combat boots, and so on.

At the theater, government officials could take a few hours off from their worries about how to end the strike in the soft coal mines, the third since the war began; or the threatened strike by the railroad brotherhoods; or the deepening shortage of gasoline despite rationing and the thirty-five mile-per-hour speed limit; or their wives' complaints about having to go bare-legged since silk was no longer available from the Orient and most nylon was going into parachutes.

By the time of the first theater intermission in New York, Colonel Shoup, sweating heavily in the burning tropic sun, had relayed a message through Maj. Gen. Julian Smith aboard *Maryland* to Gen. Holland M. Smith, who commanded all amphibious forces in the Gilberts from the battleship *Pennsylvania* off Makin Island 120 miles to the north. Shoup asked that the Corps reserve, under the control of Gen. Holland Smith and Adm. Richmond K. Turner, be released to help on Betio. Shoup concluded his message with the same words Major Schoettel had used, "Issue in doubt."

4

COTTONMOUTH BIT AND 'GATOR ET

Among the most valuable lessons we learnt from the original landings (at Gallipoli) was the folly of attempting to storm a defended beach in daylight.

Commodore Roger Keyes, Royal Navy, 1943.

The assault on Tarawa was the first attempt to storm a heavily defended beach, in daylight or any other time, since the 1915 tragedy at Gallipoli. The results of the Gallipoli action had colored the thinking of military strategists for nearly thirty years, as the quotation above from the man who was second in command of the naval forces present shows. Moreover, Commodore Keyes held that the basic strategy of Gallipoli was sound and defended this view stoutly during his long and distinguished career.

The impetus for Gallipoli came initially from the Russian government in the second year of the First World War, when Russia found itself sorely beset in the Caucasus. Their plea for a relieving action fell on the sympathetic ear of Britain's First Lord of the Admiralty, Winston S. Churchill. He proposed that a combined British and French fleet force its way through the Dardanelles Straits, and with landing parties and naval gunfire, destroy the Turkish land defenses there and, ultimately, drive that country from the war. Reinforcements and supplies could then pass through the Dardanelles into the sea of Marmara, then through the Bosporus to the Russian Black Sea ports.

On Thursday, March 18, 1915, the curtain rose on a ghastly drama of military miscalculation. Four French and five British battleships and a heavy cruiser began steaming through the narrows at the entrance to the straits in a channel reportedly free of mines. Suddenly there were gigantic explosions. Four of the battleships had struck mines. One sank immediately with almost all hands, the other ships quickly withdrew.

The commanders then decided that they needed an army. Some 78,000 British, Australian, New Zealand, and French troops under the command of Sir Ian Hamilton were hastily assembled, poorly trained, badly equipped, and loaded in total confusion aboard transports. Endless delays from inept planning gave the Turks, under the command of German Marshal Liman von Sanders, ample time to reinforce the European side of the Gallipoli Peninsula.

On Sunday, April 25, 1915, the 300-odd vessels of the attacking force stood off the southern tip of Gallipoli. Sir Sackville Carden had destroyed the southernmost Turkish forts by naval gunfire after which their demolition was completed by landing parties of sailors and Royal Marines. The Allied commanders had some knowledge of the terrain, but of the strength or disposition of the enemy forces they had none. There had been no aerial reconnaissance, no bombing of the shoreline, and little naval bombardment. The beaches were narrow, thousands of yards separated one from another, and they were surrounded by high and rugged ridges. Troops were towed to shore in open ship's boats but, because of currents, some landed in areas off their maps. Others, because of vague orders, had very little idea of what they were to do once ashore. Still others encountered stiff enemy fire from the peninsula. Of these, few got to the beach alive.

No significant inland progress was ever made, and dysentery reached epidemic proportions in the troops trapped on the narrow beaches. It was three months before reinforcements were sent. By the end of May, German submarines swarmed in such numbers that most of the fleet was removed to safer locations, leaving the troops ashore without naval gun support. Finally, in January 1916, after seven months of hell, all the Allied troops were withdrawn. Of the approximately 500,000 men committed, 250,000 were dead, sick, or wounded. Gallipoli was justly acclaimed as a complete fiasco, and hecklers still taunted Churchill about it as late as 1923. When the British government was reshuffled in May 1915, Churchill was given the lowest post in the Cabinet, minister without portfolio, as chancellor of the Duchy of Lancaster, a position from which he resigned six months later. His exceptionally promising political career, which seemed to be aimed straight at the prime ministership, had been derailed, seemingly irrevocably.

The concept of an amphibious landing on a defended beach became a military heresy shunned by nearly all strategists for the next three decades. One fruit of this general neglect was that the German forces in the autumn of 1940 were no more able to cross the narrow English Channel, despite their control of its entire eastern coast and a three-to-one numerical superiority in aircraft, than Napoleon had been 135 years before. The Corsican had said, "If we can be masters of the Channel for six hours we shall be masters of the world," but neither he nor Hitler ever achieved even this brief control. As the noted military analyst Sir Basil H. Liddell Hart pointed out in 1939, "A landing on a foreign coast in the face of hostile troops has always been one of the most difficult operations of war." This remained true even in World War II. MacArthur, who was fanatical about conserving the lives of his men, turned in a brilliant strategic and tactical performance in part by avoiding heavily contested beaches. Eisenhower's Normandy landing in June 1944 went smoothly because there was relatively little resistance along most of the Allied beaches (Omaha Beach, opposite which the Germans happened to have a division on maneuvers, was one of the exceptions.)

Most military thinkers quailed before the specter of Gallipoli, but not all. One who did not was a brilliant young Marine officer, Lt. Col. Earl Hancock "Pete" Ellis. Pete Ellis gave a series of lectures at the Naval War College as early as 1913 in which he predicted that the United States eventually would have to fight Japan and that amphibious warfare techniques would be essential in that conflict. He suggested that a program for developing such techniques be undertaken at once.

When the Treaty of Versailles that ended the First World War awarded the formerly German islands in the Pacific to Japan, both Navy and Marine planners began to think even more seriously about a Pacific war. Prior to 1920, although the Marine Corps took part in amphibious operations (largely on the island of Culebra off the coast of Puerto Rico) the emphasis was on the *defense* of islands against attack rather than offensive action against them. Then, in July 1921, Maj. Gen. John A. Lejeune, commandant of the Marine Corps, officially approved Pete Ellis's detailed program for trans-Pacific operations, designated Operation Plan 712H, "Advanced Base Operations in Micronesia." This remained Marine Corps basic doctrine for the Pacific war until the end of World War II. In it Pete Ellis had written: "Japan is a World Power and her army and navy will doubtless be up to date as to training and materiel. Considering our consistent policy of nonaggression, she will probably initiate the war; which will indicate that, in her own mind, she believes that, considering her natural defensive position, she has sufficient military strength to defeat our fleet."

The prescient young officer also wrote in 1921: "We cannot count upon the use of any bases west of Hawaii except those which we may seize from the enemy after the opening of hostilities." He went on to suggest that demolition specialists equipped with wire cutters and explosives for breaking up obstacles on the beach and in the water constitute a part of the first wave. This suggestion was ultimately made standard operating procedure —but not until after Tarawa.

Unfortunately, Pete Ellis had become an alcoholic. In 1922, General Lejeune granted him a year's leave of absence that Ellis intended to use to explore the Japanese-mandated islands. By late August, he was in Tokyo where he spent a month in the U.S. Naval Hospital in Yokohama. He was to be sent home for further treatment when, on the night of October 6, he disappeared.

Lieutenant Colonel Ellis sailed south on a Japanese ship into the area from which Japan had excluded foreign visitors. To Pete Ellis this exclusion meant that the Japanese were fortifying the islands in defiance of the Versailles treaty. He was partly right. Truk, near the center of the vast network of islands, was being developed into a powerful naval base, and airfields were being built throughout the area, for sea rescue and spotting fish, the Japanese said. The main effort to fortify the islands did not occur, however, until after the outbreak of World War II in 1939.

Ellis probably visited Truk and explored its lagoon by small boat when he was refused permission to go ashore. He then took up residence among the natives on the island of Koror, the Japanese administrative capital of the mandated islands, some 600 miles east of Truk. On the last day of his life it was simply recorded, "By nine o'clock he was roaring drunk and by three o'clock he was dead." Thus ended the life of one of the few farsighted strategists the Marine Corps ever had.

Other marines took up the work, although they ceaselessly battled obstruction from less imaginative officers. The Marines held primitive amphibious exercises in the Caribbean in the winters of 1922 and 1924. In the upper reaches of the War and Navy departments, the idea was gradually accepted that taking island bases for U.S. naval operations was a proper function of the Marine Corps. If accepted by the Navy Department this would require a large body of marines permanently attached to the fleet.

In 1933, the Navy Department created a new unit, the "Fleet Marine Force," to embody this concept. It was a great turning point in Marine Corps history that gave the Corps a new mission. By the following year, a "Tentative Manual for Landing Operations," was published by the Marine Corps Schools and became the bible for amphibious operations by all branches of the service. The Navy reissued it four years later as a Navy document, and three years after that, the Army reissued it as an Army document. Both services later turned to the Marine Corps for training in the intricacies of amphibious operations. Annual Marine Corps and Navy training exercises from 1935 to 1941 gradually evolved the necessary techniques as far as they could be developed without tempering in the cauldron of combat.

In 1935, as the Tentative Landing Manual had predicted, armor-piercing shells were found by Navy observers to be useless for ship bombardment of shore defenses. Eight years later, on the beaches of Betio, that early lesson was convincingly shown to be no longer valid.

By 1941, the Corps had an amphibious training staff in the cantankerous hands of Maj. Gen. Holland M. Smith, a tough, hard-driving perfectionist, formerly commanding general of the First Marine Brigade that had become the First Marine Division. "Howling Mad" Smith became the principal exponent of amphibious warfare. No satisfactory craft for making amphibious landings existed and Holland Smith addressed himself particularly to this need.

In 1926, Andrew J. Higgins of New Orleans had developed a boat called the *Eureka* for use by trappers and oil drillers in the shallow waters of the Mississippi and along the Gulf Coast. The vessel could be run up on river and bayou banks and backed off easily. It had both a shallow draft and a protected propeller. Repeated tests from 1939 through 1941 showed that the Higgins boat was far superior to all other craft available. After years of unfunded cooperation with the Marine Corps in trying various modifications of the basic design, Andrew Higgins's small yard got a contract to build, by the hundreds, an improved plywood model with a bow ramp that could be lowered to debark troops onto a beach. Still later models were more heavily armed and armored on the sides. Higgins, despite his flaming antipathy toward Adm. Ernest J. King, also developed the LCM; it was much better than anything the Navy Bureau of Ships had come up with for that particular job.

The amtrac (Alligator, tractor, or LVT) had a similarly torturous birth with the Marine Corps as midwife. It was first developed in 1933 for rescue work in the Florida Everglades by Donald Roebling, a retired manufacturer, to bring succor to, in his words, the "cottonmouth bit, and gator et." The Marine Corps purchased three experimental models in 1939. In 1940, after preliminary testing, the first Navy contract was given to the American Food Machinery Corporation to produce Roebling's tractors in quantity; an armored model was developed to Marine Corps specifications shortly afterwards. The original specifications included a 37-mm gun and a .30-caliber machine gun in the center turret, one .50-caliber machine gun in each side turret, and two fixed .50-caliber machine guns fired by the driver via buttons atop the two steering levers.

In parallel to the Marine development of amphibious tactics in the years following the First World War (but five years earlier since the Marines didn't really get going until 1924), the Navy began to develop the concept of naval aviation and the aircraft carrier, a development in which Adm. Ernest J. King played a crucial role. The first recommendations on the subject were issued in May 1919, barely six months after the end of the war; in the same month, a Navy plane was the first to fly the Atlantic. The first aircraft carrier, *Langley*, went into service in 1921, about the time a Bureau of Aeronautics was created in the navy; five years later, an assistant secretary of the navy for aeronautics was created. *Saratoga* and *Lexington* participated in fleet maneuvers for the first time in 1929.

All the older model amtracs (75 of 125) used at Tarawa had been developed only for cargo carrying and were unarmed and unarmored. To modify these for the tactical use to which they would be put for the first time at Tarawa, the Marines mounted machine guns forward and attempted to armor them by riveting on boiler plates scrounged from the Wellington, New Zealand, shipyards.

By the time Task Force 53 hove to off Tarawa Atoll, they expected to have 125 amtracs. The amtracs could get ashore over the reef no matter what the tide, but there were not enough of them to accommodate more than the first three waves. After that, the amtracs would have to ferry troops from the far edge of the reef to the beach, and the marines, some heavily laden with weapons or equipment, would have to transfer from one boat to another in open water and probably under fire. Moreover, most of the amtracs had already been used in the Guadalcanal campaign. Severe corrosion was beginning to take its toll. The amtracs' incredibly short service life of 200 hours had already been exceeded; some of the tractors used at Tarawa had 400 hours of operation. Amtracs would be lost if Betio were defended; even were it not, some breakdowns could be expected.

The planners had to assume that the island would be defended, and the classical ratio of attackers to defenders for such a frontal assault is at least three to one. In the unlikely event that the first three waves of amtracs reached the beach intact, the marines on the island would still be heavily outnumbered by the defenders of Betio.

If there were a single key to success in such a battle, it was for the attacking force to hit hard with everything it had before the enemy had a chance to organize its defense. So it seemed imperative that the invasion time be chosen so that there would be at least four feet of water over the reef. The Higgins boats could then pass the reef (barely, they drew at least three and a half feet fully loaded), and men and materials could be thrown ashore quickly enough to tip the balance in favor of the marines.

What were the tides of Tarawa? The answer: They were largely unknown. The atoll was far off the beaten path for commercial vessels; no tide tables for the area existed. The planners' response was to round up fifteen or sixteen men all of whom had had a professional interest in observing the tides on Tarawa Atoll for as long as fifteen years.

In most of the world there are two high and two low tides a day. The high tides are not all equally high, neither are the low tides equally low. Near the time of the new moon and again about the time of the full moon, the highest high tides of the lunar month occur. These are called spring tides. Neap tides occur just after the first and third quarters of the moon. At this time the high tides are not very high and the low tides are not very low. In other words, at neap tide the water level is low and the change between high and low tides is minimal. Because of the information gained about the tides of Tarawa, the invasion date was set back from November 15th to the 20th, reducing still further the interval before the scheduled New Year's Day landing in the Marshall Islands. For Saturday, November 20, 1943 a neap tide was predicted for Tarawa Atoll. The pressure from the Marshalls operation made it impractical to postpone Operation Galvanic for another week to take advantage of the spring tide.

There was an even more important reason weighing against postponement. The next spring tide would come either during darkness or relatively late in the day. The first would exclude air and naval gunfire support of the landing; the second would allow too little time to secure a beachhead. The next spring tide after that was a month away, less than two weeks before the scheduled landing in the Marshalls.

If the planners postponed the landing for a month it would severely restrict the time available for reconnaissance flights from Betio over the Marshalls. These flights were the reason for the capture of Tarawa Atoll. Delay could only mean higher casualties in the Marshalls. It would have meant higher casualties on Betio as well. Although the northern beaches where the marines would land were already mined, the mines were not yet armed. But Admiral Shibasaki, painfully aware of his defensive weakness on that side of the island, intended to remedy it by activating the mines and creating still more obstacles and fortifications.

In any event, it seemed unnecessary to postpone the invasion even for a week. Tide tables prepared with the help of the "Foreign Legion," as the group of Australian, New Zealand, and Fiji hydrographic advisors was called, indicated high neap tides of five feet over the reef at 1115 on November 20, with little change in maximum depth for the two days following. The "Foreign Legion" concluded, "Neap tides are variable . . . but variations from the heights given above should not be greater than one foot." The Legion called attention to a phenomenon, called a dodging tide, that sometimes occurred around Tarawa Atoll during neaps. A dodging tide has often been blamed for the difficulties encountered by the marines in landing on Betio Island. Later calculations by both the U.S. Coast and Geodetic Survey and the British Hydrographic Office show, however, that a dodging tide did not appear around Betio Island on that fateful Saturday. What did occur was an anomaly still more rare, a very small rise in the tide from its low-water level. Both U.S. and British hydrographers calculate that there was only four feet of water over Betio's reef at the high point, about 1230, that day. Although high tide was later than predicted by the Foreign Legion, its height was within the expected range.

Admiral Hill and his staff accepted the small risk of an anomalous tide (and made allowance for it by the amtrac shuttle system from shore to reef), just as they accepted the myriad other risks in the basically hazardous business of waging war. It was a cruel turn of fate that just such an anomalous tide appeared on that crucial Saturday, November 20, 1943.

5

THE BRAVE AND THE NOT SO BRAVE

The ideal defensive barrier has always been the one that could not be demolished, which held up assaulting forces under the unobstructed fire of the defenders and past which it was impossible to run, crawl, dig, climb, or swim. The barrier reef fulfills these conditions to the letter.

CincPac Operation Report, November 1943

One unit of Landing Team Two had gone into action before anyone else on D-day. This group, a Scout-Sniper Platoon of thirty-four carefully selected and specially trained riflemen under the command of Lt. William D. Hawkins arrived at the end of the long pier that formed the feet of the Betio bird fifteen minutes before the first of the main body of troops landed on Betio. With the Scout-Snipers was a squad of engineers with flamethrowers under the command of Lt. Allan G. Leslie from Oregon. The objective of the two groups was to clean out Japanese machine guns and riflemen on the long pier so that the troops coming into the beach would not be subjected to additional fire on their flanks. The Scout-Snipers and the engineer platoon did their hazardous work well, but, unfortunately, one of the flamethrowers set the pier afire while burning out a group of Japanese snipers in a small hut. The pier burned throughout the day. When the fire was finally put out a portion of the pilings had burned almost to the water line leaving a gap of thirty to fifty feet that had to be repaired before the pier could be used for bringing supplies ashore. And after Hawkins's departure the pier promptly filled up again with Japanese, and the job of clearing it had to be repeated several times.

"Hawk," as everyone called Lieutenant Hawkins, was born in Kansas, but had lived most of his life in Texas. Robert Sherrod tells us of his conversation with the twenty-nine-year-old Texan on the night before D-day. As they stood on the deck of the transport *Arthur Middleton* watching the spectacular tropical sunset Hawk said:

> You know, we're going in first tomorrow. We are going to wipe every last one of the bastards off that pier and out from under that pier before they have a chance to pick off the first wave. But one man had to stay behind to take care of our equipment. I asked for volunteers. Not a man in the crowd would volunteer to stay behind. My men are not afraid of danger.

Neither was Hawk, and his natural leadership abilities had been quickly recognized. When he first went overseas in April 1942 he was a private, first class (pfc.). On shipboard he was promoted to corporal. By the time he landed on Tulagi, a small island north of Guadalcanal on which there was severe fighting before action erupted on the larger island, Hawk was a sergeant. Less than a month later he was commissioned a second lieutenant. To appreciate that meteoric rise the reader should understand that in the Marine Corps it was usual to advance at the rate of one stripe per four-year hitch. A young man who made pfc. early in his first few years could expect to make corporal during his first six or eight years in the Corps, and so on. The pressure for NCOs during World War II speeded up the process somewhat, but the change was not spectacular.

After taking care of the matter of the pier, the slender six-foot tall lieutenant and his men could justifiably have taken it easy, but that was neither Hawk's nature nor theirs. The Scout-Snipers took off over the seawall and began dealing with the machine-gun nests and snipers behind the beach. Late in the afternoon of D-day, Hawk and a few of his men appeared on Beach Red 3 to get more ammunition. Someone yelled, "Get down Hawk, or you'll get shot." Hawk replied, "Aw, those bastards can't shoot. They can't hit anything." And he and his men, resupplied with ammunition, disappeared back over the coconut log wall.

On D-day, Hawk was wounded by shrapnel, but he paid little attention to it. The next day he hitched a ride on an amtrac that had come ashore, and standing up, he continued to pick off the island's defenders while bullets whistled around him. Single-handedly he cleaned out six machine-gun nests with two to six Japanese in each one. Then he was shot in the shoulder. He refused to be evacuated and went on fighting until he was shot again, this time in the upper chest. Later that day, Second Lt. William Deane Hawkins died of his wounds. He was awarded the Congressional

Medal of Honor; one of four gained by the Second Marine Division on Betio.

Robert Sherrod also talked to Dr. Edwin J. Welte, a crewcut young Minnesotan five years out of medical school. Dr. Welte remarked that, "Nobody is trying to get out of this battle." Of the whole battalion aboard *Arthur Middleton*, only eleven men were in sick bay, five with recurrent malaria. The others had had minor accidents and one marine suffered from a chronically bad back. Dr. Welte was killed as his boat moved toward the Betio beach.

On Beach Red 3, Maj. Henry Pierson Crowe had a hot fight on his hands as the afternoon of D-day wore on. When he had told his men of their assignment the major said: "And for the third beach—that's Red Beach Three—they've picked this battalion—and you all know me." His marines whistled and applauded to show their approval both of their assignment and of their formidable leader. Now Crowe and his men were in a vicious fight. Men were being killed or wounded every minute and Crowe and his executive officer, Major Chamberlin (later wounded), were busily trying to make order out of chaos.

To the left of Crowe's position was the long tail of the island from which the defending Japanese could move against his narrow beachhead at will. By late afternoon, Major Crowe could count more than fifty disabled tanks, amtracs, and boats in the water on both sides of the long pier. Even dead Japanese were dangerous. A sniper was driven from a pillbox fifteen feet inland of the log barricade by a charge of TNT and killed instantly by a burst from a flamethrower that reduced him to charred bones. For a full minute afterwards, however, the bullets in his cartridge belt exploded and sang their lethal song over the heads of the marines crouched along the seawall.

The plan was to run the amtracs inland before unloading the troops but only two got past the seawall. Crowe had two half-trac 75-mm guns but both broke down early. He got all four of his medium tanks ashore, but by evening only one was left. Colonel Shoup had gained lateral contact with Crowe at an early hour and three medium tanks arrived near where Shoup set up his command post about the same time as he got ashore.

At Second Battalion headquarters, Lt. Col. Walter Irvine Jordan, originally attached to the battalion as an observer, took command after Colonel Amey's death. Colonel Jordan told the marines gathered against the seawall to move forward because their help was needed inland. A few went, but many stayed huddled in relative safety behind the log barricade. "They don't know me, you see," Colonel Jordan explained to Robert Sherrod. "They haven't got the confidence men should have in their officers."

Other young marines could not be stopped. A spindly kid, not more than eighteen, blond before the dirt and blood got into his hair, came down over the seawall on Beach Red 3 on that first morning. His whole left ear was slashed to ribbons and half his face with it. He crouched, dazed and shaking, while a Navy doctor slapped a big sulfa bandage over his torn head. He would not lie down, he just sat there stroking a bloodied rifle, his blue eyes jumping with pain. After a little while he asked for a drink of water and, having had it, made ready to leave. "Better lie down," someone said. "Ah, fuck that!" said the kid in a husky voice, spitting blood. "I gotta get back to my outfit." He climbed back up over the log seawall and disappeared into an area on the left flank where a fierce fight was raging.

By midafternoon, Lt. Col. A. F. Johnson went up on a scouting mission with Lt. (jg.) F. C. Whaley in one of *Maryland*'s planes. Whaley made several passes over the island at treetop height, so low that Colonel Johnson could read the license numbers of a pair of Japanese civilian automobiles, but they saw almost no Japanese troops. The marines were as naked as newborn babes to the defenders' fire while the Japanese prudently stayed put and fought from their well-protected positions.

By then, Colonel Shoup had established communication with Crowe and Major Ruud on Beach Red 3; with Lieutenant Colonel Jordan on Red 2; with Maj. Wood B. Kyle, who had come to help Jordan but was still afloat in the lagoon; and with Maj. John Schoettel. Schoettel—whose nerve seemed to have failed him—was still off Beach Red 1 in an amtrac and out of contact with his troops, so he could give Shoup no information about the situation ashore. After a message to that effect was sent to Shoup from Schoettel the reply came directly to Major Schoettel from Gen. Julian Smith. It gave some clue as to how the seemingly gentle, dreamy Julian Smith had become a Marine general. The answer was short and brutal: "Direct you land at any cost, regain control your battalion and continue the attack."

Major Wood Kyle was then ordered to land the First Battalion, Second Marines on the left edge of Beach Red 2, then turn west to make contact with Schoettel's men on Red 1.

The situation on Beach Red 1 was actually better than anyone expected. Major Michael P. Ryan had taken command of a wildly mixed assortment of troops, many of whom were supposed to be somewhere else (Beach Red 2), but who had been driven west by the fierce fire from the Japanese strong point between Beach Red 1 and 2. One of the men was Maj. Howard Rice, who had been Lieutenant Colonel Amey's executive officer. Major Rice brought a rich dowry to Mike Ryan—a radio that worked. Rice had tried to land on Red Beach 2 but was driven to Red 1 instead. With him came Navy Lieutenant Thomas N. Green, a gunfire spotter who had his radio with him. This permitted Ryan to make contact with Colonel Shoup around sunset and apprise him of the situation on Beach Red 1.

The news was good. Ryan, his motley crew, and two medium tanks had gotten ashore and driven south from their original perimeter on the western end of the island. By late afternoon of D-day they had advanced through an area about 500 yards deep and 150 yards wide. Then they ran into intense fire from Japanese emplacements, and Ryan had neither demolitions nor flamethrowers. Besides, they had bypassed Japanese troops concealed in their rear, and these popped up to harass stretcher bearers, medical corpsmen, and Marine infantrymen when least expected. The Japanese snipers were made more formidable by the fact that Japanese smokeless powder was much better than the American version. Their positions were not betrayed by telltale wisps of smoke after they had fired their rifles.

Late in the afternoon Major Ryan prudently pulled back to an area that he thought he had a good chance of defending during the night.

The unarmed stretcher bearers and medical corpsmen were heroes of a very special kind. Marine bandsmen (called "field musics") exchanged their musical instruments for stretchers in combat and had the dangerous job of carrying the wounded from the front lines to areas where they could more effectively be given medical attention. These men, running erect with a loaded stretcher, were easy targets; many were killed or wounded. The Navy medical corpsmen, similarly unarmed, tended the wounded where they fell. They also supervised their transport to rear areas, sometimes escorting rubber rafts loaded with wounded out into water deep enough to accommodate the Higgins boats, and then waded back through the perilous shallows to do the job all over again. A man with a weapon felt that he had at least something of an equalizer, even if it was only a carbine; he could fight back by emptying a clip of bullets in the general direction of a sniper or a gun emplacement. But it took a rare kind of courage and devotion to go defenseless into that hail of fire on errands of mercy and to repeat the journey over and over.

Solomon Kozol, a small, slender man, was a Navy lieutenant serving with the Eighth Marines as a dentist. He went ashore to treat facial wounds and ended up carrying wounded men on his back out to the amtracs and carrying water and ammunition to the front lines until a Japanese bullet shattered his right arm, paralyzing it. Kozol was probably one of a very few dentists to win both a Silver Star and a Purple Heart in World War II.

Communications failures were a leitmotif running through the entire operation against Tarawa Atoll. Every salvo from *Maryland* completely knocked out her communications for a variable period of time, and *Maryland* was the communications hub of the entire operation.

At the other end of the communications chain, in the various Marine units fighting ashore or waiting in landing craft for their turn to go ashore, things were even worse. They were totally reliant on two types of combat radios, the TBX and the TBY. Both were cumbersome and heavy; neither was waterproof. The TBX was generatorpowered, so somebody had to crank it. The TBY was batterypowered but weighed fifty pounds. The marine's combat pack had to be worn by radiomen below the TBY. The combat pack was put on suspenders so that it reached approximately to the marine's backside where it slapped back and forth at every step. Needless to say, the "ass pack" was universally detested. In addition to these aggravations the radiomen had to contend with the risk of being heard by the enemy when the TBX generator was being cranked or of being located when they raised their antennas to transmit. Since Operation Torch in North Africa the year before, the Navy had been complaining about the radios given them, but BuShips (as the Navy's Bureau of Ships was known) had not yet provided better equipment.

Many sets were knocked out permanently by shell fragments or bullets; most of the remainder refused to work after they got wet, which in an amphibious operation happened frequently. By patiently drying out the dampened sets and cannibalizing wrecked sets for parts, the Marine radiomen kept some semblance of a communications network going. Still, there were repeated occasions where communications failed totally between the flagship; Colonel Shoup's command post; and the various units scattered along the beach, in the lagoon, and outside the reef. The landing craft had portable radios but most of them were promptly shot out or drowned out and this contributed to the chaos in the lagoon and in the staging areas around the transports.

One fantastic communications foul-up occurred shortly after Gen. Julian Smith had gotten permission from Gen. Holland Smith to use the Corps reserve (the Sixth Marine Regiment). This development made it possible for Julian Smith to commit the First Battalion, Eighth Marines to the eastern end of Beach Red 3 (Major Crowe's left flank) to help guard that exposed area against counterattack by the Japanese forces on the eastern end of the island (the bird's tail).

Long before noon on D-day, gray-haired Col. Elmer E. Hall, a former mining engineer who commanded the Eighth Marine Regiment, had begun to get the men of the First Battalion, Eighth Marines into boats in order to be ready to go ashore. Shortly before two in the afternoon they were ordered to the line of departure. In midafternoon, Gen. Julian Smith's headquarters aboard *Maryland* radioed Colonel Shoup asking,. "Do you consider a night landing by LT 1/8 (under the command of Maj. Lawrence C. Hays, Jr.) suitable and practical on Beach Green? If not, can reinforcements land on Beaches Red 2 and 3 after dark?"

Beach Green was the western end of Betio, the sloping, tufted head of the Betio bird (see the map of Betio Island, situation at 1800, D+2). A landing there would have reinforced Major Ryan's vigorous attack and then swept eastward along the airstrip and the heavily defended south beach. Colonel Shoup never answered this important question from his commanding officer because he never received it. Finally, in late afternoon, General Smith, who had become increasingly concerned with the situation of Beach Red 3, sent a message to Colonel Hall ordering him to land Hays's battalion on the extreme eastern end of the north beach at 1745 hours, just one hour and twenty minutes after the message was sent.

Considering the probable concentration of Japanese troops on the eastern end of the island, Hall's men were being sent to certain destruction, but General Smith was gambling that the move would prevent the entire beachhead from being rolled up by a counterattack from the eastern end of the island. Had this happened, most of the marines ashore would have been killed or captured and the invasion of Tarawa Atoll would have been a total failure.

The crucial order from General Smith was acknowledged aboard the transport *Monrovia*, but Colonel Hall was not there. He was in a landing craft near the minesweeper *Pursuit* waiting for orders to land, and he expected these orders to come to him via *Pursuit*'s radio shack. His own radio never picked up General Smith's message, and if *Pursuit* picked it up, it was never relayed to Colonel Hall.

About half an hour later, this drama took another amazing turn. Colonels Johnson and Edson, in division command headquarters, asked the observer aboard the *Maryland*'s number one observation plane to watch the line of departure and report any movement of boats from that area. If Colonel Hall's boats left the line of departure it would show that he had received the message although he had not acknowledged it. As the observer, Lt. Col. Jesse M. Cook, watched, an artillery battery of the First Battalion, Tenth Marines left the line of departure and headed toward Beach Red 2 where they had been told to land. How a single battery of 75-mm pack howitzers* could have been mistaken for an infantry battalion is not clear, but at the time the lagoon was crowded with vessels going in all directions in utter confusion, and this probably contributed to the difficulty of making an accurate report. In any case, the report reached Gen. Julian Smith that Colonel Hall's unit was moving toward Beach Red 2 (rather than toward the eastern end of the island where they had been ordered to go), and it was so plotted on the situation map in division headquarters. It was midnight before General Smith learned that Colonel Hall and his weary men were still bobbing uncomfortably at the line of departure waiting for orders.

The adventures of *Maryland*'s number one observation plane were not yet over. About 1830, after two hours in the air, the pilot, Ens. G. K. French, requested permission to be taken back on board *Maryland*. By then the fleet was expecting an air attack since Japanese planes were attacking U.S. ships only thirty miles to the west (an action discussed in more detail later.) French's request was denied since *Maryland* might have to take vigorous evasive action in the event of such an attack and she would be immobilized

---

*This weapon had been designed by the Army to be carried in pieces to the battlefield by mules and then assembled. The marine innovation was to replace mules with marines.

during the act of transferring her observation plane from the sea to the plane's perch on deck.

French flew off to the north and then returned toward the fleet flying only 300 feet over the water. The nervous gunners on shipboard assumed that it was an enemy plane and opened fire. Fortunately their shooting was not accurate; it seldom was. French landed his plane in the water, which suddenly seemed a good deal safer than the air, and he and Colonel Cook spent a miserable night afloat on the ocean. They returned to *Maryland* the next morning.

The first marine to win the Congressional Medal of Honor on Betio was S. Sgt. William J. Bordelon of Texas, a member of an engineering platoon (First Battalion, Eighteenth Marines). The island's defenders drew a bead on Bordelon's amtrac as it neared the beach. Twenty-five men were aboard. Four got to the beach alive. Unfortunately for the Japanese, one of them was Bill Bordelon. Once ashore, he quickly made up two demolition charges and personally disposed of as many enemy pillboxes. As the marines were to learn to their sorrow, however, the underground positions were divided into chambers so that a flamethrower blast, a grenade, or a satchel charge thrown into one gun port did not necessarily disable all the others. Sergeant Bordelon was hit by machine-gun fire when he attacked a third pillbox but he stayed on his feet, snatched up a rifle and covered another group of marines who were scaling the seawall. Then, after refusing medical attention, he waded into the surf to rescue two other demolition men who were wounded and calling for help. After he got them ashore, this incredible man, bleeding profusely from several wounds, went after another pillbox. But Bill Bordelon's luck had run out. He was stopped by a blizzard of bullets and died instantly.

As the afternoon of D-day wore on, one of the two tanks that had greatly assisted Major Ryan's advance on Beach Red 1 was put out of action, and shortly after, the second tank was hit and burned. The first tank, named *China Gal*, commanded by Lt. Edward Bale from Texas, still had a working machine gun and it was used as a fixed-gun emplacement to protect Major Ryan's flank as night settled over the atoll. Of the fourteen medium tanks that had left the LSD (Landing Ship, Dock) that morning, only one was fully functional. *Colorado,* under the command of Lt. Louis Largey of California was on Red 3 helping Crowe's men deal with Japanese emplacements. Lou Largey had started out in *Cannonball* but had his radio knocked out twenty-five yards from the beach. Largey waded ashore but Crowe told him to go back to his tank. Then *Cannonball* was hit by a shell and plunged into a crater. Largey spent six hours getting back to Marine lines and then took over *Colorado. Charlie* and *Condor* were blown up and Largey finally took *Colorado* out to the reef to the abandoned tank and took spare guns and ammunition. All the crew of *Cannonball* were wounded so he picked up a new crew and went back to work on Red Beach 3.

Lieutenant Colonel Evans F. Carlson, who had led the raid on Makin, was present on Tarawa as an observer, and he wound up in Colonel Shoup's command post on beach Red 2. Carlson, a tall, slender man, reminded some of Abraham Lincoln. He had enlisted in the Army at sixteen. By World War I he was a captain on General Pershing's staff. After a brief stint as a civilian he enlisted again, this time as a marine and, after a year, was a commissioned officer.

Shortly after noon on D-day, Colonel Shoup asked Carlson to make a trip out to *Maryland* to explain the situation ashore and Shoup's immediate plans to General Smith. Carlson was first given permission to take an amtrac out to the end of the pier to bring some of Major Ruud's battalion to Red 2. Carlson made several such trips, then left his amtrac at the reef's edge and took another boat out to *Pursuit.* There he transferred to a boat going to the transport *Zeilin* from which he caught another boat to the flagship. Colonel Carlson finally arrived at division headquarters about midnight.

While Carlson was ferrying troops ashore, Gen. Julian Smith told his second in command, Brig. Gen. Leo D. "Dutch" Hermle, to take a small staff and put them into boats and prepare to land on order. He was later instructed to proceed to the end of the pier, assess the situation, and report to Julian Smith by radio.

On the way to the pier, General Hermle radioed Shoup asking for the location of Shoup's command post, but received no answer. At 1740 Hermle radioed division headquarters that he was at the end of the pier and was under fire. A quarter of an hour later he again attempted to contact *Maryland* but failed and finally sent a messenger out to one of the ships to transmit his message on to *Maryland.* Major Stanley E. Larson, Major Ruud's executive officer, was pinned down under the end of the pier and was out of contact with Ruud. Hermle finally made intermittent contact with Shoup and learned that the marines on Beach Red 2 were running out of ammunition and water. Hermle contacted Larson and directed him to have his men carry ammunition and water in to the beach as they advanced. The general also set up a traffic flow of wounded marines going in the opposite direction. Hermle had been in irregular contact with Major Crowe on Beach Red 3, but at 1930 communications with the beaches failed totally. Hermle then sent two of his officers to find Shoup's headquarters and to get advice from Shoup on where and when reserves should be landed.

From the end of the pier to Shoup's command post was a mere 600 yards or about two city blocks, but it was 600 yards of sheer hell since it was swept continually by Japanese machine-gun and antiboat fire. Hermle's officers accomplished their mission but it was nearly four in the morning of D+1 before they returned. General Hermle now had his information but no way of sending it directly to headquarters. His only course of action was to go out to the destroyer *Ringgold* and transmit his information from there.

A group of engineers, meanwhile, put out the fire on the pier and, about midnight, began repairing the damage. Even at night it was a fearfully exposed position and casualties were heavy, but the job was done. The surface of the pier was of white coral grit. After 0100 when the moon came up, and with the additional light from the inferno ashore, the men on the pier were perfect targets for the Japanese gunners ashore. But, once the pier was fixed they continued to go back and forth bringing in supplies from the end of the pier.

At 0445, Leo Hermle radioed Julian Smith recommending that Hall's unit, still bobbing in the lagoon, be sent ashore close to the pier. The message was never received. Smith had sent Hermle a message shortly after his arrival at the end of the pier; it directed him to take over command from Colonel Shoup so that the colonel could get some much needed rest. Neither was this message received, and Colonel Shoup remained in command ashore for another day. Meanwhile, because messages from ashore continued to bear Colonel Shoup's name it was feared in division headquarters that General Hermle and his staff might have been killed.

Colonel Shoup continued to ask for ammunition, water, plasma, and other military and medical supplies. They were being sent ashore in a steady stream from the transports, but there was no record that it was being received. Finally, Maj. Ben K. Weatherwax was ordered ashore from *Monrovia* to locate Shoup or Hermle and find out what was happening to the supplies. Weatherwax reached the pier about 2100 on D-day when General Hermle was still on the seaward end of the pier. Weatherwax, however, landed on the beach side of the gap burned in the pier earlier in the day, and he never learned of Hermle's position. Weatherwax did find Colonel Shoup and he got the necessary information about supplies. He then tried twice to get the word back to *Monrovia* by radio, but failed. He finally went back to the transport, arriving there shortly after dawn of D+1.

All during D-day the transports, anxious to be gone before enemy planes or ships appeared in force, vigorously continued unloading. The result was that the lagoon and the area seaward of it were soon filled with more than 100 landing craft loaded with supplies that nobody wanted at the moment, the movement of badly needed equipment and troops was choked off because of a shortage of boats. Only amtracs could get to shore, and these were increasingly in short supply as old age and enemy gunfire took their toll. The amtrac battalion commander, Maj. Henry Drewes, had been killed, and this added to the confusion.

By evening of D-day, the position of the marines ashore was precarious.

About 5,000 men were on land, but one of every three was dead or wounded. By then there had been thirty-two air strikes against targets specified by the ships, shore parties, or *Maryland*'s spotter planes.

What these strikes meant to the men ashore was described by Coast-guardsman Carl Jonas who found his section of the beach suddenly under intense fire by newly positioned guns and under imminent threat of counterattack (or so it seemed at the time). Then:

> A plane floated over us very low, a Kingfisher . . . tipping first on this side and then on that to get us in his field of vision. He circled off and was gone. Whatever it was going to be it was decided.
>
> It happened almost immediately. A holocaust dropped from the sky, our fighter planes strafing and searing . . . the Japanese. From far to the right came the deep, whooming blast of naval gunfire, and the whole Jap side of the island seemed to rise in splinters and flame. . . . Then we knew our Marines were advancing. We began to breathe again.

That night *Ringgold* anchored in the lagoon, *Anderson* cruised off the south side of the island, and *Frazier* off the west end to provide on-call fire for the marines throughout the night. On Beach Red 3, Major Crowe's left flank was naked to counterattacks from the eastern end of the island that, if successful, would spell the end of the invasion. General Julian Smith's efforts to reduce this threat by using Colonel Hall's men as a diversion had floundered in the morass of communications failures.

The marines had no continuous line. The defensive perimeter, such as it was, consisted of little groups of men in shell holes, captured trenches, and some covered positions in dubious communication with one another. The western flank of Red 3 and the eastern flank of Red 2 were in occasional contact, but between Red 2 and Red 1 there was a 600-yard gap controlled by the Japanese strong point that threatened the flanks of both Marine units. The degree of disorganization that existed is shown by the roster of men with whom the commander of Company F (2/2) found himself: six men from Company F, sixteen from Company E, and fifteen from Company H.

Ever since noon, Julian Smith had been trying to get help for Crowe's vulnerable eastern flank on Red 3. He had ordered Major Ruud and his Third Battalion, Eighth Marines ashore to land on Crowe's left. Japanese fire from that area was so savage that Ruud's men angled to the right away from it. When Major Ruud arrived on the beach in late afternoon he found that the organization of his battalion had been shattered. Many of his commissioned and noncommissioned officers were missing, and most of the men were badly shaken by their ordeal and incapable of fighting effectively. Instead of being moved to Crowe's dangerous left flank, Ruud's men were left on the somewhat less dangerous right flank where the intense Japanese fire had driven them.

Some artillery had been landed. On Beach Red 3 the marines had somehow gotten two 37-mm guns ashore but were stymied because there was no break in the seawall through which they could be dragged and placed to bear on the Japanese positions. This logistical problem was solved when a marine saw two mustard-colored Japanese tanks rolling toward the beach. Both 900-pound guns were suddenly lifted by many willing arms up and over the seawall, almost as if they had suddenly sprouted wings, and they were instantly positioned, trained, and fired at the approaching tanks. One tank was disabled, the other prudently withdrew to search for less well-armed targets.

Elsewhere the marines had brought ashore 75-mm pack howitzers in pieces and assembled them on the beach at Red 2, and a few 81-mm mortars had been brought ashore on Red 2 and 3.

Colonel Shoup's command post on Beach Red 3 was behind a big Japanese bunker. There were still a dozen Japanese inside, but Colonel Shoup simply posted sentries at the entrance to keep them there and went calmly about his business.

Later, the men dug foxholes for the night. Half of them slept while the other half stood guard against the counterattack they were certain would come. Properly carried out against the slender American positions an attack could hardly help but succeed. Many a marine on Betio was certain that the gorgeous sunset of D-day was the last he'd ever see.

After dark, things were much quieter. The rubber tubes of Japanese gas masks, plentiful on Guadalcanal, had been sliced up by the marines to form rims for dog tags so the noise of the two tags banging together would not give away their owner's position. The Japanese pink tracers occasionally arched over the beach and toward the pier. And some of the marines noticed something else. From seaward, the reddish orange of American machine-gun fire was coming in on the beach. It didn't make sense! Then someone realized that the Japanese had sent men out to the abandoned tanks and landing craft and were turning the guns on the beleaguered forces on the narrow strip of beach. That was adding insult to injury, but there was little the marines could do about it until morning. By then it might no longer matter.

As night fell, the lines of wounded stretched for yards along the beach. The "smoking lamp" was always out at night on Betio, the flare of a match or the glowing tip of a cigarette could alert a Japanese sniper. It was hard on all the marines, but hardest of all on the wounded who were deprived of so much else. There was no morphine, no plasma, no food, not much water, and little ammunition. The marines on Betio were no longer an effective fighting force because of lack of supplies. All along the beach wounded marines died slowly, white-faced and in searing pain, and nothing could be done to help them. Their buddies could only lie in their shallow foxholes waiting for the Whump! of Japanese mortars beginning to shell the narrow beach in preparation for the inevitable counterattack.

6

PORTRAIT OF PARADISE
WITH SHEEP

For a while in 1942, the Second Marine Division had its three regiments (the Second, Sixth, and Eighth) together on Guadalcanal. Then, the Second Marine Regiment and the First Battalion, Eighth Marines began boarding ships for New Zealand on the morning of January 31, 1943. Many of them, debilitated by tropical diseases and months of combat, had to be carried aboard. Early in February, the Second and Third battalions of the Eighth Marine Regiment, Second Division began leaving the 'Canal, and the Sixth Regiment boarded transports some two weeks later.

In the Second Division, about half the men had had malaria and risked further attacks of the disease at any time. A number of men had contracted dengue (bone-break) fever, another debilitating, mosquito-borne disease, along with fungus infections that flourished in the tropical climate of Guadalcanal. Some had filariasis, which, if untreated, could lead to the grotesque swellings of elephantiasis in which a man's leg or scrotum could swell to many times its normal size and stay that way.

The marines of the Second Division were tired and sick, but their first glimpses of New Zealand's North Island lifted their spirits. The first thing they saw, from many miles at sea, was the symmetrical bulk of Mount Egmont, "New Zealand's Fujiyama," rearing more than 8,000 feet above the surface of the sea. The Second Regiment arrived in summer and found it warm, but most of the Sixth and Eighth regiments arrived when the cool breezes of autumn were still blowing. For all the marines, there was the thrill of approaching Western civilization again as the transports swung first into Cook Strait separating the North and South islands of New

Zealand, and then continued their roughly circular course until they came alongside the piers in Port Nicholson, the vast and well-protected harbor of Wellington, the capital city of New Zealand. It is a spectacularly beautiful place. Hills rise sharply from all around the harbor, and on most of them, gaily-painted houses rise in tiers so steep that the roof of one two-story house nearly reaches to the foundations of the one above. New Zealand had even more to offer than its own considerable natural beauty. The New Zealanders (Kiwis they were called) knew that the marines had suffered and died on Guadalcanal so that the previously unstoppable Japanese drive to the south could be halted before it overran Australia and their own islands.

Even before Guadalcanal, the marines had been well received by the Kiwis. General Archer "Archie" Vandegrift tells of his arrival in Wellington to begin planning, on very short notice, for the invasion of Guadalcanal. He was horrified to learn that Marine headquarters would be in the Hotel Cecil, a very old building in downtown Wellington. The building was perfectly satisfactory, but it was also fully inhabited, largely by older people. "No problem there," responded the New Zealand liaison officer when General Vandegrift questioned him, "They'll be out in forty-eight hours."

"You're planning to evict those people on our account?"

"Righto," the liaison officer replied, "This is the only possible place for you." He went on to explain to the incredulous general that the occupants understood the nature of the emergency and would not resent transfer to other quarters. Archer Vandegrift was not convinced.

The very next day, after the conversation with the liaison officer, General Vandegrift was stopped on a Wellington street by an elderly, stern-looking gentleman with a clipped white moustache who asked, "You are the American general?"

"Yes. I am General Vandegrift."

"Well, sir, I am very glad to meet you. I want you to know, sir, that I have lived at the Hotel Cecil for twenty-six years."

Vandegrift braced himself for what he thought was coming. He was astonished when the old man suddenly smiled and said, "I want to tell you sir, how pleased I am to move from my apartment so that you and your officers have a place to do your job."

That incident made General Vandegrift realize that he had come to a very special place. The Kiwis, many of whose own young men were fighting and dying in the deserts of North Africa and elsewhere and who were suffering under very strict rationing, nevertheless opened both their hearts and their homes to the war-weary men of the Second Marine Division, and the marines responded gratefully.

One jarring note in the otherwise splendid relationship between the Kiwis and the marines was sounded when General Vandegrift first arrived in New Zealand prior to the invasion of Guadalcanal. He found that New Zealand's stevedores, in addition to taking morning and afternoon tea breaks, didn't work when it rained. Since it rains on 150 days of an average year in New Zealand this meant that ships were unloaded with glacial slowness. General Vandegrift solved this problem by unloading his ships with his own men, and the marines worked rain or shine for a day and a night. There was much wailing and gnashing of teeth at the stevedore's union headquarters, but they found little support from the government of the islands.

New Zealand's animal population included about two million dairy cattle. In the first few days after the various groups of marines arrived at Wellington that number seemed barely adequate. One thing that few servicemen in the Pacific theater ever had was fresh milk. Even those who did not care much for milk under normal circumstances acquired a passion for it that the insipid powdered milk did nothing to slake. The thirsty marines nearly drank the creameries of Wellington dry. Not surprisingly, there are milk bars all over the city, and they did a thriving business in ice cream sodas, milk shakes, chocolate milk, and plain milk; milk in any form was consumed by the marines as if they never expected to see it again, and many never would.

Milk wasn't the only thing the marines liked about Wellington. They liked the steak and eggs that the Kiwis were fond of for breakfast. They liked the brisk air and the turbulent traffic. They learned to like roast lamb and, with a bit more effort, warm Waitemata beer and an Australian concoction named Corio. The marines called Corio "jump whiskey" because, they claimed, one drink would make a man jump like a kangaroo.

The marines, however, never became enthused about a ghastly green alcoholic beverage from Mexico called Juarez that was advertised as "high-class Scotch," and was only barely fit for human consumption. The marines, who would drink anything alcoholic, or that they thought might be alcoholic and was not instantly lethal, drank Juarez anyway, but they complained mightily about it. And they complained mightily about the fact that New Zealand pubs—following the barbaric custom of the mother country—closed at 10:00 P.M. Not surprisingly, the marines liked the women of Wellington, and their interest was frequently reciprocated. Some 500 marines married Wellington girls in the nearly nine months that some of the men were there.

No place in Wellington was large enough to accommodate the entire division. The 15,000 men of the three infantry regiments moved to a camp called McKay's Crossing near the community of Paekakariki about thirty-five miles north of Wellington. Other units encamped at Titahi Bay, in Judgeford Valley, and at Pahautanui, only eighteen miles from Welling-ton. Before they left in November, many of the marines had even learned to pronounce the Maori place names that dotted the New Zealand landscape.

Wounded and sick marines went directly from the ships in Port Nicholson to the Second Division hospital at Anderson Park or the Navy Hospital at Silver Stream near the Hutt River that flowed into Wellington Harbor.

After several weeks of few responsibilities, it became time for the Second Marine Division to settle down and get back to work. A number of replacements had come out from the United States, and these had to be integrated into the division's traditions; a forty-mile forced march was a common initiation.

On May 1, fifty-eight-year-old Gen. Julian Smith took over command of the division. Smith had joined the Corps as a second lieutenant in 1909. He had served all over the world and he had won the Navy Cross, that service's highest decoration, during his service in Nicaragua. His footlocker was full of decorations from South American governments.

General Smith was not the sort of fire-eating Marine general whom Hollywood loved to portray. He was friendly, unassuming, and his concern for his men was deep and genuine. But his face, with its hooked nose and sharply chiseled jaw, radiated authority, and "General Julian" could be a hard man when the situation required it. He would not have been a Marine Corps general otherwise.

For his chief of staff, Julian Smith had Col. Merritt Edson, winner of the Medal of Honor at Bloody Ridge on the 'Canal. They were a pair of opposites who worked well together. When General Julian smiled his whole face seemed to glow, and his whole body exuded warmth; only Colonel Edson's mouth smiled. General Smith was a brilliant planner and an inspiring leader. Colonel Edson had some of those qualities, too, but mostly he functioned as a tough-minded taskmaster. Between them they got the Second Marine Division whipped back into shape for the toughest job in its history.

Although the pace of training gradually picked up, there was still time for fun. The marines learned to consume another New Zealand delicacy called "shell shock," composed of one-third port wine and two-thirds stout. Eleanor Roosevelt visited the island, shook hands and talked with many of the wounded men, and conveyed from the American people their gratitude to the people of New Zealand for their kindness to the battle-scarred marines. To many of the marines, the peripatetic wife of their president was a figure of fun before they met her. When they met her they saw what they already knew from the newsreels and newspapers, she was not a physically attractive woman. When she spoke they learned that her voice was harsh. But by the time she had departed they had forgotten all that and remembered that they had talked to a woman of immense warmth, intelligence, and personal charm.

There were occasionally USO. (United Service Organization) shows from the States, dances, trips to New Zealand's many spectacular outdoor areas, and even weekly hunting trips for shots at New Zealand's considerable deer population. These trips were arranged by Lt. Col. Alexander Swenceski who later saved his life by climbing to the top of a pile of dead marines on Betio's beach.

In September, the winds from the Antarctic that had brought winter to New Zealand began to give way to the gentle breezes of spring, the pace of training quickened, and the marines began to sense that something was coming up.

The U.S. Army had driven the Japanese out of the Aleutians and had taken New Georgia in the Solomon Islands northwest of Guadalcanal. General Douglas MacArthur had also inched his way along the northern coast of New Guinea. In July, Adm. Chester A. Nimitz, commander in chief, Pacific and Pacific Ocean Areas, had issued an order to plan for a Central Pacific offensive against the Japanese, and Churchill and Roosevelt, at the Quadrant Conference in Quebec, had adopted the plan of the U.S. Joint Chiefs of Staff for a trans-Pacific drive toward Japan.

The following month Vice Adm. Raymond A. Spruance visited Gen. Julian Smith in Wellington and brought the word that to the Second Marine Division would fall the honor of striking the blow against the Imperial Japanese Navy's most heavily fortified position in the Gilbert Islands. The conquest of Tarawa Atoll would make possible operations first against the Marshall Islands, then against the Marianas, from which strikes could be made against the Japanese home islands themselves.

Late in September, Smith and his staff flew to Pearl Harbor to present their plans to the command of the Fifth Amphibious Corps (usually called 5th 'Phib) of which Smith's division had recently become a part. In New Zealand, the already brisk pace of training speeded up even more. The marines again filed aboard transports to sail north to Hawke Bay and elsewhere on North Island to practice amphibious landings. The Second Amphibian Tractor Battalion under Maj. Henry Drewes was especially busy. Amtracs had previously been used only for supply and rescue missions. Now they were practicing assault landings while live ammunition was fired over the tops of the little vessels. But nothing could quite prepare the amtrac's crews for the hell of Tarawa.

Meanwhile, when their duties permitted, the marines continued to instruct the women of Wellington on the differences between the various units of the Second Marine Division. The alleged differences were usually derogatory to the units other than that to which the speaker belonged. The Sixth Regiment of the Second Division had won fame in France during the First World War at Château Thierry where they provided the stiffening that permitted the French Army, reeling backward under savage German attack, to regroup and halt the German advance. Less than a week later, they fought for and secured Belleau Wood where they took nearly 1,100 casualties in twenty-four terrible hours. A grateful French government awarded the Sixth Regiment the left shoulder *fourragère* as a symbol of the regiment's distinctive service.

This loop of mostly green braid worn by the men of the Sixth Regiment was usually referred to by the other marines as "chicken guts," and they solemnly assured the Kiwi women that it meant that the wearer had a venereal disease.

Other marines pointed out that the Sixth was universally referred to in the Corps as the "Pogey bait" Sixth. They explained to the mystified Kiwis that the Sixth had acquired that appellation while en route to Shanghai in the 1930s. The regiment's men, so the story went, had bought thousands of candy bars (Pogey bait) from ships' stores, but only two cakes of soap. Pogey was Navy and Marine slang for children; Pogey bait was what you used to get children to shine your shoes, do your laundry, or whatever. The marines usually managed to convey the impression that the men of the "Pogey bait" Sixth used Pogeys for such unspeakable sexual exploitation that the upright and God-fearing men of other regiments could not begin to describe it in mixed company.

The much-maligned Sixth wasn't the only Marine unit about which derogatory tales circulated. One battalion of the Eighth Regiment had been composed of Marine reservists from the Los Angeles area. This battalion had provided a suitably martial background for a number of movies. They were naturally referred to as "The Hollywood Marines," with the obvious implication that they were composed of equal parts of tinsel and celluloid, and therefore not quite real. The term "Hollywood Marines" was often extended to cover the entire Eighth Regiment, most of whose members had never seen a movie set.

This was all good, clean fun so long as one member of a unit of the Second Marine Division or "2ndMarDiv" applied these derogatory terms to another unit of the same division. But woe to any soldier or sailor who spoke ill of any part of 2ndMarDiv or the Marine Corps generally. He was apt to find himself in the center of a brawl no matter which unit of the division he was with at the time. Criticism by outsiders was not welcome. The heavy-buckled belt of the Marine uniform was a formidable weapon whether used as a club or as a substitute for brass knuckles; the Navy countermeasure was a short piece of lead pipe sewn into the uniform's neckerchief. Soldiers usually had enough sense to stay out of brawls between those two branches of the U.S. Navy, which had been at logger-heads since 1775.

As September wore on, marines and their ladies who strolled along Lambton Quay on a spring evening knew that there was a reason Port Nicholson was filling up with ships, and it became clearer when the big Marine camps began to be struck. There was a constant scurrying of harassed officers in and out of "K room" on the third floor of the Hotel

Cecil that looked down over Lambton Quay and the harbor. In this room, guarded twenty-four hours a day, the invasion of Tarawa Atoll had been planned. The official story, for the benefit of Japanese agents (if any), was that the marines were only going on maneuvers to Hawke Bay on the east coast of North Island. Arrangements were made for rail transportation of the men back to the Wellington area camps, and with the New Zealand Air Force to provide air cover for the landings. Few of the marines, and probably even fewer of their wives, were fooled, however.

2ndMarDiv began boarding their sixteen transports in the harbor on October 28, and all equipment and men were on board by Halloween. Before dawn the next morning the transports began edging out of the bay; the steep hills of Wellington dropped slowly astern. Most of the men knew from past experience that Hawke Bay was only a day's trip by transport from Wellington. By dawn of November 2, even the most stubborn marine had to admit that the Hawke Bay story was a red herring. If they still remained unconvinced, their last illusions were shattered when the convoy grew and grew as destroyers came up over the horizon and then took station alongside.

By the night of November 6 the old salts in the convoy could smell land. Only a few of the officers and none of the men knew what that land was, but the next morning they were there. It was a large, fertile, and flattopped island called Efate in the New Hebrides, some 400 miles west of Fiji. Efate possessed, among other advantages, the substantial anchorage called Havannah Harbor. It was filled with U.S. Navy warships, among them the battleship *Maryland*. Admiral Richmond Kelly Turner commanded the "5th 'Phib," in sometimes uneasy collaboration with Maj. Gen. Holland M. Smith. Kelly Turner's deputy, a tall, slender, and handsome naval gunnery expert and student of amphibious warfare, Rear Adm. Harry Hill, moved his flag aboard *Maryland*. So also did Gen. Julian Smith, whose relationship with Harry Hill was the exact counterpart of Holland Smith's with Kelly Turner, but much less rancorous.

Colonel William M. Marshall had overseen the rebuilding of the Second Marine Regiment in New Zealand after the Guadalcanal experience. Now, on the eve of the battle for Tarawa Atoll, Colonel Marshall, who was to command ashore on Betio, became ill and had to be relieved. Julian Smith took a chance and promoted his able operations officer, Lt. Col. David M. Shoup, to full colonel on the spot, and asked Shoup to take over for Marshall. It was a risky thing on the eve of battle, but Shoup more than lived up to General Julian's trust in him.

2ndMarDiv had left Wellington on sixteen transports and acquired a destroyer division as escort soon after. Early on the morning of November 13 the transports moved out of Mele Bay in which a couple of practice landings had taken place. From Havannah Harbor came the battlewagons *Maryland*, *Colorado*, and *Tennessee*, the heavy cruiser *Portland*, and the light cruisers *Birmingham, Mobile,* and *Santa Fe.* Trailing along with these great ships came a less imposing, but equally essential, trio: the minesweepers *Requisite* and *Pursuit,* and the LSD *Ashland,* pregnant and near term with a womb full of General Sherman tanks. It was a weeklong voyage, tedious and uncomfortable. Fresh water was available on the transports for one hour in the morning and one hour in the evening, and the marines could then shave, or wash clothes or themselves out of wash basins or buckets. The showers were saltwater in which the marines washed with large brown bars of "saltwater soap" that resolutely refused to lather. If they were lucky they could rub themselves down after a saltwater shower with a towel moistened with fresh water. If not, the saltwater left their skin feeling sticky for the rest of the day, but, since they sweated profusely in the tropical heat, which was especially unbearable below decks, a little additional salt from the shower probably added little to their discomfort.

As always, rumors—nourished by boredom—abounded. "The word" quickly ran through the transports. "It's going to be Wake." That bubble burst four days later.

On November 14 Admiral Hill had the following signal flashed to the transports. Sixteen signalmen on the sixteen transports quickly wrote down the message as it came from the blinking signal light on the bridge of the transport. "Da-da-dit, dit-dit, dit-dit-dit-da, dit"—and so the story ran. "Give all hands the general picture of the projected operation and further details to all who should have this in execution of duties. . . ."

The big maps and models came out of their previously guarded cabins, and the island they showed looked nothing like Wake. Its code name was Helen, and on its northern beaches there were three zones marked Red 1, Red 2, and Red 3.

The first waves of amtracs approach the beaches of Betio
Island, Tarawa Atoll, on the morning of D-Day.

First wave of amtracs approaching Beach Red 3. The long pier
separating Beach Red 3 from Red 2 is in the background.

A painting by marine combat artist Sgt. Tom Lovell showing a later wave disembarking from a broached Higgins boat and wading ashore to Beach Red 3.

(left) At high tide a marine wades ashore toward Beach Red 3 alongside the long pier.

(below) Marines leave their tiny beach and climb over the seawall under heavy fire.

A group of marines advance along Beach Red 3 toward the pier. Two wrecked amtracs have been abandoned at the water's edge.

Marines encircling the sand-covered Japanese fortification, seen in the right background.

A squad leader points out the Japanese position that is holding up their advance.

A marine counting "Mississippi One, Mississippi Two" as he prepares to throw a grenade (with a four-second fuse) from behind a sandbag wall. Yankee marines who thought that even one Mississippi was too many could count two Alligators before pitching the grenade.

Marines assault the large, bombproof emplacement just inland from the pier.

A bulldozer strips the sheet metal and coconut logs from atop a Japanese fortification so that the marine engineers can demolish it with gasoline or explosive charges.

Marines wounded on a rubber raft are escorted by "field musics" and navy medical corpsmen out to where they can be picked up by a Higgins boat and taken back to the transports. Despite their general antipathy to the U.S. Navy and all its works, most marines had nothing but praise for the Navy corpsmen who accompanied them, unarmed, into battle.

A dozen of Betio's staunch defenders lie dead in the sand.

A sturdy pillbox finally neutralized by explosives and flamethrowers.

Wrecked amtracs and marine bodies in the water just beyond the seawall attest to the bitter price paid for Betio Island.

A closer view of amtrac #44 impaled on the seawall on Beach Red 1, her bow a network of bullet holes. What is apparently a wrecked Japanese light tank lies in the background. Three dead marines are in the water beside the amtrac.

This and following pictures show the strength of the Japanese defenses of Betio Island. This row of antiboat obstacles on Green Beach is extended in the background by a high fence.

This coconut log fence on Green Beach was meant to channel landing craft into areas swept by antiboat guns. Fortunately, the Japanese had not had time to similarly fortify the northern beaches where the marines initially landed.

The massive construction of the 8-inch gun emplacements is clearly shown in this photograph.

A heavy machine gun emplacement inland on Betio Island. The weapon could be fired in any of three directions, and the emplacement was virtually impervious to anything but direct assault with flamethrowers and demolitions.

An 80mm coast defense gun poised to fire over the beach. The pile of shell casings shows that it was heavily used in attempting to repel the marine invasion.

(left) A tank trap, only half revetted, extending across much of Betio Island east of the air strip.

(below) This steel and concrete blockhouse was Admiral Shibasaki's command post, and it became his grave. The symbol of the Japanese Special Naval Landing Force is on the sunlit side of the blockhouse. One edge is against the shadow of the fallen tree.

Two of the 8-inch guns brought from Singapore.

A marine shares his water with a kitten found cowering under a wrecked Japanese light tank alongside the Japanese command post.

Disabled marine amtracs await salvage at the junction of Beach Red 1 and 2.

Dead Japanese troops sprawl beneath palm trees.

7

A Sweet Sunrise

It's sweet to see the sun rise when you expected to die in the dark, and the sun rose on schedule over Tarawa Atoll on Sunday, November 21, 1943. To their surprise, most of the marines clinging to their slender beachhead on Betio were alive to see it. Many of the wounded had died during the night, but there were few additional casualties during the hours of darkness. And, although there had been a nuisance air raid by a single Japanese plane just before dawn, the feared Japanese counterattack had not come.

Nevertheless, the marines' situation on that Sunday morning was unwholesome. On the western tip of the island, the beak of the Betio bird, Major Ryan's mixed troops held a roughly triangular area about 300 yards deep. Two sides of the triangle extended to the water on the southern end of Green Beach (the crested head of the Betio bird), and about an equal distance along Beach Red 1. The remaining three-quarters of Beach Red 1 and about half the adjacent Beach Red 2 remained firmly in Japanese hands; from this area, the defenders could pour withering machine-gun and antiboat fire onto Beaches Red 1 and 2.

Marines held half of Red 2 and Red 3, but the forces holding the two positions were in poor communication. The marines on both beaches had extended their control about 300 yards inland from the long pier. They held about half the triangle enclosed by the airstrip and its two taxiways, but all forces were exceedingly short of food, water, ammunition, and medical supplies.

The defenders had been busy during the night. They had moved machine guns in to bear on the forward Marine positions close to the airstrip, and they had men installed in a sunken freighter offshore and in the wrecked or abandoned tanks and landing craft that dotted the reef. During the night they had also plugged the hole that had allowed some marines to cross the taxiway. By the morning of D+1 machine guns were placed to fire down the long axis of the taxiway, and no one could expect to cross it alive. Moreover, the morning of the twenty-first was to bring a normal tide, unlike the abnormally low tide of D-day, and this higher tide brought with it the threat of drowning for the wounded marines lying on the beach.

As Robert Sherrod wrote just before dawn of D+1:

> 0530. The coral flats in front of us present a sad sight at low tide. A half dozen marines lie exposed, now that the water has receded. They are already one-quarter covered with sand that the high tide left. Further out on the flats and to the left I can see at least fifty other bodies. I had thought yesterday, however, that low tide would reveal many more than that. The smell of death, that sweetly sick odor of decaying human flesh, is already oppressive.

White-haired Col. Elmer Hall, commanding the Eighth Marine Regiment, had spent nearly twenty hours in a landing craft near the line of departure waiting for orders to land. With him were his headquarters group and the First Battalion, Eighth Marines. Finally, at 0200 Sunday morning (D+1) he received a message asking where he and his men were and what condition they were in. He replied that they were resting easy in their boats at the line of departure near the minesweeper *Pursuit*. Another two and a half hours went by. Then Hall received a message ordering him to make a diversionary landing on the eastern tip of Betio. These were the same orders that had been sent him the day before, although they had never reached him.

If Colonel Hall realized that he and his men were being sent to almost certain death to take the pressure off Red Beach 3 and abort the threat of counterattack, he gave no evidence of it. He went ahead planning the landing, which was to be made at 0900, and the setting up of a new line of departure well to the east of the line he then occupied.

Meanwhile, at 0513, General Hermle, now on the destroyer *Ringgold*, radioed to division headquarters that Colonel Shoup wanted Hall's men to land on Beach Red 2. A few minutes later. Hall was told to land at once on Beach Red 2. Once ashore, his men were to attack to the west, against the Japanese strong point, and attempt to link forces with Ryan's men on the beak of the Betio bird.

At 0615 on D+1, the first wave of the First Battalion, Eighth Marines, under Maj. L. C. Hays, Jr., climbed out of its boats onto the reef, about 500 yards out, and began to wade to the beach. Like their predecessors, they were soon caught in the Japanese meat grinder. Casualties were heavy. Hays's men lost all their flamethrowers, all their demolition devices, and most of their heavy equipment on the way to the beach—precisely those things essential in assaulting the Japanese strong point—and they reached the island badly shaken and disorganized.

The previous day, when Lieutenant Colonels Carlson and Rixey were on their way to the beach they had discovered that there was a relatively safe corridor into the northwestern lagoon coast. As Carlson described it: "The only approach to the beach that was relatively secure was a corridor about 100 yards wide which extended west from the pier." Carlson later wrote of the landing by Hays's men:

> The unit sustained heavy casualties on the way in. The hulk northwest of the pier contained snipers and machine gunners. As I waited off the pier for an amphibian tractor, planes came over and got four direct hits on the hulk, and in so doing strafed the wounded of the First Battalion, Eighth [Marines] who dotted the water nearby. Apparently the commander of the First Battalion, Eighth Marines was not aware of the 100-yard corridor west of the pier. In fact those on the water off the beaches at this time were uncertain of the situation ashore and were even under the impression that the enemy had reoccupied the pier.

Robert Sherrod was also watching Hays's men make their fiercely disputed landing on Beach Red 2.

> The machine guns continue to tear into the incoming Marines. Within five minutes I see six men killed. But the others keep coming. One rifleman walks slowly ashore, his left arm a bloody mess from the shoulder down. The casualties become heavier. Within a few minutes I count at least a hundred Marines lying on the flats... 0730:... There are at least two hundred bodies which do not move at all on the dry flats, or in the shallow water partially covering them. This is worse, far worse than it was yesterday.

The historian Samuel Eliot Morison also remarked on the ordeal of Hays's battalion:

> In order to avoid one field of fire, some Marines waded into the cove of Beach Red 1 . . . where they were shot down almost to a man. During the five hours or more that Major Hays's men required to complete landing their losses were greater than those of any other battalion that landed on D-day.

Hays's battalion lost 331 men killed and wounded out of 800, most of them on the reef. The Second and Third battalions, Eighth Marines who landed on Beach Red 2 on the previous day took about the same losses, but these were incurred in fighting their way inland; there were almost no casualties taken on the way to the beach. Nevertheless, the 400 of Hays's men who made it gave Shoup the added power he needed to begin to turn the tide.

The Navy crews of the Higgins boats pulled wounded marines from the water. One Navy gunner silenced an enemy machine gun with his vessel's .30-caliber gun, worked over a wrecked landing craft to kill a Japanese sniper there, and then joined the rescue party.

Morison quotes Lt. E. A. Heimberger:

> The cool, impeccable seamanship of this boat's unidentified coxswain was admirable. He kept perfect control of his boat against a strong current, holding her off the wounded men and yet close enough to lift them from the water and not ground the boat.... Finally the last of the wounded men, 13 in all, were lifted into the boat, leaving about 35 men in the water, unharmed as yet but without rifles. They refused to come into the boat and asked this officer (Lt. E. A. Heimberger) to bring them back something to fight with. The coxswain backed out while bullets were zinging about his head and the men on board were stamping out incendiary bullets which threatened to ignite his cargo of drummed gasoline.

Private, first class James Collins of Spartanburg, South Carolina, landed with the First Battalion, Eighth Marines, according to Robert Sherrod:

> The water was red with blood. All around me men were screaming and moaning. I never prayed so hard in my life. Only three men out of twenty-four in my boat ever got ashore that I know of.

By 0800, Major Hays had about half of his men ashore. The rest of the morning was spent getting them organized and positioned for the attack to the west.

The vigor of the small-arms fire that greeted the dawn of D+1 convinced Colonel Shoup that the action was going to continue at about the same level as on the previous day. He hoped to split the enemy forces in two and directed the First and Second battalions, Second Regiment that held the positions nearest the Japanese airstrip to advance toward the south side of the island, to attempt to cross the airstrip, and take the formidable defenses of the southern beach from behind.

Colonel Shoup had been running the battle ashore for more than twenty-four hours, and he was tired, wounded, and irritable. At 0825 he radioed *Maryland*: "Imperative you land ammunition, water, rations, and medical supplies in amtrac on Beach Red 2 and evacuate casualties."

This was easier said than done, no matter how imperative it might be, and Shoup's orders to the First and Second battalions, Second Marines were not easily carried out either. Crossing the island required, as had the advance of the day before, that two or three men work their way forward in front of their unit until they were close enough to throw a hand grenade into the enemy bunkers or pillboxes that formed interlocking chains blocking the Marine advance. Alternatively, the marines could attempt to riddle the bunker's interior with automatic-weapons fire or to blow it up with blocks of TNT tied together and thrown into the entrance or gunslits. Yet another technique used flamethrowers to burn the defenders out of their fortified positions. When loaded with four gallons of napalm, a flamethrower weighed up to seventy-two pounds and consisted of a wand and three tanks, one containing compressed air, the other two fuel. Usually the flamethrower valve was turned with the right hand and the trigger igniting the charge with the left. Air drove the flaming napalm out of the wand at tremendous pressure. If the marine carrying the flamethrower failed to lean forward to counteract the "kick" at the moment of opening the valve he would find himself on his back drenched with napalm and about to be incinerated by his own weapon. It happened more than once. Since two hands were needed for operation, the men carrying the flame-throwers were otherwise unarmed. They had to work their way forward while being covered by riflemen until they could spray a pillbox entrance with fire, then take cover, if there was any, while the riflemen mopped up.

If these methods worked, alone or in combination, then a platoon, or what was left of them, could move forward a few more feet. The Japanese defenders knew well enough what methods the marines used to overcome fortified positions, and they were indefatigable in trying to prevent their loss.

Later in the morning of D+1 carrier-based planes came over the island and bombed and strafed the area south of the airstrip to soften it up for the Marine advance.

About noon of D+1, Lt. Col. Walter Jordan, who had taken command of 2/2 after Colonel Amey was killed, reported to Colonel Shoup that he had repeatedly sent out runners to contact his southernmost troops since he had no radio contact with them, but that none of the runners had reported back. Colonel Shoup, his aggressiveness unstilled, and perhaps even heightened by his aggravations, ordered Jordan to move his command post toward the south beach and reestablish contact with his men.

On the western end of Betio, Maj. Mike Ryan moved his men southward along Green Beach, the crested top of the head of the Betio bird. At the southwest corner of the island the Japanese had emplaced twelve antiboat guns and two naval turret five-inch guns. This concentration of weapons was protected with numerous machine-gun positions and rifle pits. Most of the antiboat guns and both the five-inch guns had been put out of action by naval bombardment, but Major Ryan felt that more naval gunfire on the Japanese positions was desirable before he tried to capture the area.

Navy Lieutenant Thomas Green, serving with the Marines, called in the fire of two destroyers, and shortly after 1100 Ryan and his melange attacked with the support of the two repaired medium tanks in addition to the guns of the destroyers. The Japanese offered little resistance to Ryan's advance, and before long, the entire length of Green Beach was in Marine hands.

On Beach Red 3, however, Major Crowe and his men were stymied. In front of their lines not far from the beach was a steel reinforced emplacement, inland was a large bombproof shelter. Several attempts to destroy the steel emplacements on both D-day and D+1 had led to heavy casualties. The Second Battalion, Eighth Marines had no better luck in the direction of the airstrip. The day was largely spent in strengthening the battalion's position in preparation for the next day's action.

Lieutenant Colonel Evans Carlson reached Colonel Shoup about midday and found him in low spirits. Shoup reiterated his determination to stick and fight it out, but more than stubbornness and courage were needed, and the situation was, if anything, worse than on the preceding day. Others concurred: "At no time during the morning of the second day was there any reason for optimism on the part of division (Gen. Smith and his staff) or Colonel Shoup."

Shoup told Carlson that his greatest needs were water and ammunition, and he asked Carlson to return to *Maryland* with that information. On his way back to the command vessel, the industrious Colonel Carlson and Lt. Col. C. J. Salazar, the shore party commander, set up a shuttle of the remaining eighteen available amtracs (of 125 that began the battle some thirty-six hours before) to move the most-needed supplies to the beach. The tractors took wounded men from the beach to the end of the pier and returned with supplies brought to the pier by the Higgins boats. The Higgins boats then took the wounded out to the fleet and returned with more supplies.

Meanwhile, back aboard *Maryland*, Gen. Julian Smith called a conference at 0900 to discuss how the Sixth Marines he now had in reserve might best be used. The outcome of the meeting was that Col. Maurice G. Holmes, commanding the Sixth Marines, was directed to send a strong force ashore in rubber boats to Green Beach South, immediately. Colonel Holmes chose the First and Second battalions to make the landing, and they set about making their preparations to do so.

At 1022 that morning, division headquarters had sent a message to Shoup asking if he had sufficient troops to complete the occupation of Betio. Shoup replied that the situation ashore did not look good. Robert

Sherrod reached Colonel Shoup's headquarters behind the Japanese pillbox at 1100. He later wrote: "Colonel Shoup is nervous. The telephone shakes in his hand. 'We are in a mighty tough spot,' he is saying."

Major John Schoettel, who had finally gotten ashore on the evening of D-day but had not yet rejoined his unit, sent Shoup a message at 1133 that troops who had attempted to land on Beach Red 1 had been driven back to their boats by heavy machine-gun fire.

About that time Sherrod was with the men of H Company, the heavy weapons company of the battalion with whom he had come ashore. The man sitting next to him in an alleyway between an uncompleted wooden barracks and a tier of coconut logs set up around it to protect the building from shrapnel told him, "We've already had fifteen men killed, more in twenty-four hours than we had on Guadalcanal in six months. And I don't know how many are wounded."

Around noon correspondent Sherrod returned to Shoup's command post just as Major Schoettel came up in tears. The young man said plaintively: "Colonel, my men can't advance. They are being held up by a machine gun." Shoup, almost dizzy with fatigue and the pain of his now infected wounds, spat into the sand, "Goddlemighty, one machine gun." Later John Schoettel, thoroughly miserable, returned. "Colonel, there are a thousand goddamn Marines out there on that beach, and not one will follow me across to the airstrip." Colonel Jordan, now back at the command post as an observer spoke up, "I had the same trouble. Most of them are brave men, but some are yellow." Colonel Shoup, in spite of his condition, gave his officers a lesson in leadership: "You've got to say, 'Who'll follow me?' And if only ten follow you, that's the best you can do, but it's better than nothing." As another officer later described it to Admiral Morison: "We are not all heros. I started inland with about 100 Marines to take out a machine gun that was giving us trouble, but by the time we got there there were only two or three with me."

There was action elsewhere on Tarawa Atoll on D+1. Company D, Second Tank Battalion was the division's scout company. On D+1 the First, Second, and Third platoons of this company landed on various parts of the atoll. Buota, the islet that makes the bend at the elbow of the atoll had a Japanese position estimated to contain 100 enemy sailors of the Special Naval Landing Forces. There was also a radio station. On Eita the scouts found fuel, bomb and mine dumps, but no Japanese. Just after dark that night the Japanese forces moved through the positions of the First Platoon undetected.

Shortly after midday of D+1, division headquarters queried Shoup again about conditions on Betio Island. At 1214 he replied in chilling words: "Situation ashore uncertain."

8

RENGO KANTAI

The rifleman's world on Betio was often a circle perhaps a dozen yards across encompassing a Japanese fortification in front of him, his buddies on either side, and the wounded and dead marines behind him. For Colonel Shoup the universe was a space a couple of miles in diameter that included all of Betio Island and its lagoon and extended to the flagship *Maryland*. To Gen. Julian Smith and his naval counterpart Adm. Harry Hill, and to the captains of the lightly armed transports, the world extended to the nearest Japanese air bases at Mili in the Marshall Islands, about 300 miles away, to Nauru in the eastern Gilbert Islands, and beyond them to the Japanese military nerve center in the Pacific, the great naval base at Truk in the Caroline Islands to the northwest.

As Radio Tokyo had put it two weeks after the fall of Guadalcanal: "No fleet of battleships supported by carrier-based aircraft can successfully attack vital points within the range of Japan's land-based aircraft." The Japanese Army spokesman, Colonel Yahugi, affirmed that: "The innumerable islands scattered throughout the vast Pacific Ocean have become land bases (that is, bases for land-based planes), and as a result . . . we hold absolute supremacy within the strategic sphere of these bases." And behind this defensive ring the Combined Fleet, the mighty *rengo kantai*, stood poised to crush any forces that might penetrate the perimeter.

The Japanese scheme to repel an invasion in the Gilbert Islands (of which Tarawa was a part), was a portion of a larger design called the Z plan. An attack on the Gilberts would be met first by long-range aircraft from the Bismarck Islands (particularly Rabaul some 800 miles away) that would attack the American forces, then fly on to land at fields like Mili, or at other airfields farther north in the Marshall group. Short-range aircraft would move through Truk and then on to fields like Mili and Nauru from which they could move against the invading forces. This last phase would require some four days, but the Japanese planners did not consider that to be a problem. Based on their forces' previous performance, they expected Tarawa to hold out for a long time no matter what force was thrown against it.

While long-range aircraft were making the initial response, the Z plan called for a fleet of six or seven submarines, usually based in the Bismarcks to move into the Gilberts and attack the warships and transports there. The coup de grace would be administered by the powerful Japanese Combined Fleet moving swiftly down from its home base at Truk.

Harry Hill and Julian Smith had had one bit of luck, if a carefully planned and brilliantly executed operation could be called luck. Admiral Isoroku Yamamoto no longer commanded the Combined Fleet, his mantle had been assumed by Adm. Mineichi Koga, whose gifts were much more limited than those of his predecessor.

In April 1943, the commander in chief of the Combined Fleet had decided to visit Japanese bases in the upper Solomon Islands. Admirals Halsey and Nimitz learned of Yamamoto's intentions and Nimitz asked the top U.S. intelligence officers a vital question: "Would the elimination of Yamamoto help our cause?" The answer was a resounding "Yes!" Japan had no officer who could take his place. Many U.S. naval officers knew Yamamoto personally, and they had a high regard for him as an intelligent and resourceful leader.

At 1100 Sunday, April 18, Yamamoto and his most important staff officers boarded two Betty twin-engined bombers at the strong Japanese Navy base at Rabaul in the Bismarck Islands. When Yamamoto's schedule was settled one of his officers took it to Eighth Fleet headquarters and asked to have it transmitted by courier. The communications officer insisted that it be sent by radio. "No," said Commander Watanabe, who had brought the message, "It might be picked up by the Americans and decoded." The communications officer was adamant. The code had only gone into effect shortly before, and, besides, it could not be broken. The message was sent by radio. Shortly afterward the message was picked up by Combat Intelligence in Pearl Harbor. After working all night, the Navy intelligence group had Yamamoto's schedule in plain English.

The two bombers carrying Yamamoto and his staff were protected by nine Zeros on the 250-mile flight to Kahali airstrip on the southern tip of Bougainville. The Bettys and their escort arrived over Kahali airstrip at 1135. Sixteen twin-tailed P-38 Lightnings of the 339th Fighter Squadron, U.S. Army Air Force, led from their home base on Henderson Field, Guadalcanal by Maj. John W. Mitchell, arrived over Kahali at the same time.

As the two Bettys began to drop onto the runway at Kahali, the escorting Zeros turned away—and the Lightnings pounced. Captain Thomas G. Lanphier shot down one bomber, Lt. Rex T. Barber got the other. The first, which carried Yamamoto, crashed into the jungle, the other carrying Yamamoto's chief of staff, Vice Admiral Ugaki, spun into the ocean and sank. Yamamoto and five or six key staff officers were killed, Ugaki was critically injured. Only one American plane was lost.

Yamamoto was found still strapped in his seat, his left hand grasping his sword, his head lolling foward as if he were asleep. A bullet had passed through his lower jaw and out through his forehead, a second bullet had passed into his chest from his left shoulder blade. He had written Chioko on the evening of April 2: "Tomorrow I'm going to the front for a short while. . . . I shan't be able to write for about two weeks, so don't worry, will you? April 4 is my (sixtieth) birthday. I feel happy at the chance to do something. Well then, take care of yourself and good-bye for now."

The reaction was best expressed by Japanese Vice Admiral Fukudome. Everyone knew that there "could only be one Yamamoto and nobody could take his place." His loss "dealt an almost unbearable blow to the morale of all the military forces." A few days before his death Yamamoto had written: "I am still the sword of my emperor. I will not be sheathed until I die." When he was dead the Japanese pilots asked: "Who will lead us now?" and thousands gathered to watch the train with his ashes as it carried the remains toward Tokyo. Still more thousands gathered to visit the spot where his ashes were kept on the afternoon of his state funeral.

The death of Yamamoto, posthumously named a fleet admiral, was a blow to the Japanese armed forces, but it did not render the Combined Fleet impotent. On November 1, 1943 the Third Marine Division, along with New Zealand and U.S. Army units, had landed against light initial resistance at Cape Torokina, the northern end of Empress Augusta Bay on Bougainville. Although there were some 50,000 Japanese troops on the huge island, only 270 men defended Cape Torokina. By nightfall, the marines had 14,000 men ashore. From the northern tip of Bougainville the great Japanese naval base of Rabaul was only 170 miles away and Japanese headquarters reacted vigorously while the Allied troops ashore were still in a vulnerable position. The first Japanese air attacks arrived six minutes after the first marines hit the beach, 55 planes in the first group, about 100 in the second group that arrived two hours later. And just before 0300 on D+1 the Japanese Torokina Interception Force of two heavy and two light cruisers and six destroyers was only nineteen miles from the cape when they were intercepted by Rear Adm. A. Stanton Merrill with four light cruisers and eight destroyers.

Merrill's plan for the Battle of Empress Augusta Bay was to place his cruisers across the entrance to the bay and prevent the entry of a single Japanese ship. Five hours later Merrill's force, victorious in the naval engagement, was attacked by more than 100 Japanese planes. For the first time in the Pacific war since General Doolittle's strike on Tokyo, U.S. carriers emerged from an all-out attack without damage. This was because the slow Wildcat F4F had been replaced by the speedy Hellcat F6F and the Corsair F4U—the Japanese planes had not been improved significantly since the war began—as well as because of better American antiaircraft protection, radar, and ship handling. On D+5 on Bougainville a huge Japanese force of nineteen ships, including seven heavy cruisers and one light cruiser, and 270 planes was massing at Rabaul to strike against the American invasion force. Rear Admiral Frederick C. "Ted" Sherman made the risky decision to send two valuable carriers against the powerful base since there was nothing else to send. Ninety-seven planes from the carriers *Saratoga* and *Princeton* put that Japanese fleet out of action, and many of the same planes struck at Japanese aircraft based at Rabaul six days later. Only then was the beachhead on Bougainville reasonably secure from sea and air attacks that could have driven the Marine invaders back into the sea. No Japanese heavy cruiser ever bothered Bougainville again.

All this was known to Admiral Hill and Gen. Julian Smith. It was encouraging, but although the Japanese forces had been badly cut up, they remained a formidable force. Still at Truk, and in full fighting trim, were the two huge battleships *Yamato* and *Musashi*, the smaller battleships *Nagoto, Fuso, Kongo,* and *Haruna,* the heavy cruisers *Kumano, Chokai, Suzaya,* and *Chikuma,* five light cruisers, eighteen submarines, and a large number of destroyers.

Time was of the essence. Tarawa had to be securely in American hands within about three days. Otherwise, the supporting naval forces might have to withdraw to fight a naval battle against a powerful Japanese force from Truk. That would leave the marines ashore with little further air or sea support and with the possibility, if the American forces got the worst of a sea fight, of having Japanese warships and transports sailing up to Betio Island to pin the marines against the upper and nether wheels of an enemy millstone. By noon Sunday, November 21, 1943, half the allotted three days had gone by, and as Colonel Shoup had said, the situation ashore was still uncertain.

The Army Air Force, Navy, and Marines had taken all the measures they could to weaken Tarawa's defenses and to reduce the Japanese ability to wage a powerful sea or air attack against the American transports and the troops ashore. Some of these precautions had started months before.

Although the marines on Betio would have said that the little island was already overpopulated with defenders it might have been much worse. Patrolling close to Jaluit, an island east of Mili in the southern Marshalls on May 20, 1943, Comdr. B. E. Lewellen, skipper of the U.S. submarine *Pollack,* noticed two Japanese patrol craft. Suspecting that bigger game was afoot, Lewellen waited. His patience was rewarded when the 5,400-ton auxiliary cruiser *Bangkok Maru* appeared in the *Pollack*'s periscope. Aboard her were 1,200 troops bound for Tarawa. They never got there. *Pollack* blew the stern off the *Bangkok Maru* with four torpedos and half of her passengers went to the bottom with her. The rest, without weapons or equipment, got ashore on Jaluit where they spent the rest of the war. There was another large Japanese vessel in the vicinity, but *Pollack* never saw her. It was that ship that brought the eight-inch guns from Singapore to Tarawa Atoll. Other Japanese troops also scheduled to go to Tarawa were diverted later to Bougainville and elsewhere in the Solomons to meet Allied threats in those areas.

The carrier-plane strikes against Tarawa from *Lexington, Princeton,* and *Belleau Wood* in mid-September were mentioned earlier and, as D-day neared, such strikes became more frequent and more intense. Mili, Jaluit, and other airfields in the Marshalls were hit repeatedly at the same time, and many Japanese aircraft were destroyed. These attacks were carried out first by U.S. Army Air Force Liberators and, later, by carrier planes from the new *Lexington,* the new *Yorktown,* and the light carrier *Cowpens.* The Army's Liberators also worked over Betio.

General Julian Smith had proposed landing Marine artillery on the unfortified island of Butaritari, next to Betio in the Tarawa Atoll, and using that artillery to bombard the Japanese positions. That plan was ruled out because of time considerations. For the same reason, no prolonged naval bombardment of Betio could be allowed since this would tip off the Japanese to where the assault would come. At this point the clock would start running, and every tick would bring the Japanese Combined Fleet that much closer to Betio. Betio had to be taken by surprise and by storm. The emphasis on speed was made clear by the ammunition allowance brought up for the marines on Tarawa Atoll. The total available was sufficient for only *five* days normal consumption (five units of fire), and this included allowances for waste and possible loss of one or more of the cargo ships carrying munitions. Betio would have to be taken quickly or the game was up, although few of the commanders cared to think about the second alternative.

Fortunately, the secret of the American attack on Tarawa was well kept by the simple expedient of sending air strikes against a number of possible targets and by the naval forces approaching the area on courses that seemed to be taking them somewhere else, then altering course for Tarawa Atoll under cover of darkness on D-1. It was not until carrier planes struck heavily at the airstrips on Nauru and a Japanese scout plane sighted the ships of the Northern Attack Force that Tokyo guessed what was up and began shifting reinforcements and sea and air forces into the area.

The first air counterattack on the Gilberts force came on the evening of D-day. At 4:25 on that afternoon a lookout aboard the light carrier *Independence* about thirty miles northwest of Tarawa sighted a submarine periscope. Captain R. L. Johnson ordered the ship to flank speed (twenty-five knots) and signaled to Rear Admiral Montgomery that he had seen a submarine. A destroyer went to investigate while Johnson resumed his previous course and speed a few minutes later so he could recover his antisubmarine planes that were coming home for the night. Then the telephone rang on the bridge—the combat information center below decks, where the radar plotting was done—reporting a large group of unidentified planes coming in from the west and low over the water. This was a standard Japanese tactic for torpedo bombers. They attacked from the west late in the day so the setting sun behind them was in the eyes of the gunners aboard ship, and they came in low to avoid radar. This flight, however, had been seen by a member of the antisubmarine patrol as he was getting ready to land. Captain Johnson, his heart pounding a little faster, put down the telephone, looked west—and there they were—fifteen Bettys off the starboard beam and coming in fast.

The klaxons shrieked General Quarters and *Independence* became a scene of purposeful chaos. Running feet pounded the decks and the watertight hatches were shut and dogged down to stop the flow of water from compartment to compartment if the hull were holed. For some of the crew whose battle stations were below the waterline there was always a thrill of fear as the watertight doors were closed and sealed from the outside—if the sea entered their compartments they probably would drown at their posts.

Far above them, in the warm afternoon sun, the line of Bettys suddenly altered course away from the rest of the ships and headed straight toward *Independence*. Captain Johnson promptly turned *Independence* twenty degrees to port (left) to both present his narrow stern rather than his broad flank to the enemy and, at the same time, to get closer to the rest of the fleet so their antiaircraft fire could augment his own.

Three of the Bettys quickly split from their formation to pass in front of *Independence* to head her off. Captain Johnson ordered a fast turn to starboard and then, after the planes had passed, back to port. The maneuver had brought the three Bettys within range of the destroyer *Hale*; she promptly shot down one of them.

But *Independence*'s troubles were not yet over. As Johnson watched with satisfaction as the crippled Betty crashed into the sea, a lookout on the bridge spotted a torpedo wake on the starboard quarter. The Japanese torpedos could make nearly fifty knots, almost twice the carrier's maximum. *Independence* was firing everything it had and getting hits, Bettys splashed into the sea, shot down by the ship's gunners, three of them just 100 yards away. But by then four torpedoes were streaking toward the carrier. Three passed harmlessly astern, one passed close along the starboard side. Those of the carrier's crew who had been watching the wakes breathed a quick sigh of relief at the misses just before a fifth torpedo hit the ship just aft of the funnel on the starboard side, blowing a fighter off the flight deck and a starboard twin 44-mm gun tub and crew across the flight deck and into the water on the port side.

On *Oakland*, twenty-four-year-old Signalman 1st class Robert Boulton, like the rest of the crew, was fighting back with everything he had. Stationed on the after bridge near the second funnel, he fired some seven clips from a BAR at the attacking planes. Then he became *Oakland*'s only casualty from the action: when the ship made a high speed turn, he slipped on the empty shells on the deck, and inadvertantly grabbed the redhot barrel of his BAR, severely burning his hand.

Meanwhile, stricken *Independence* began listing to starboard, eventually reaching twelve degrees as fires started here and there in the after part of the ship. The damage control party went quickly to work. The list was eventually reduced to three degrees, and the fires were put out. The ship could no longer be steered from the bridge so the steering station was moved aft. Most of the crew in the lower battle stations had been brought up, although some were lost when their compartments were flooded. *Independence*, with destroyer escort, started back for American waters, which she ultimately reached safely. *Independence* had seventeen men killed and forty-three wounded; her after engine room, fireroom, and magazine were flooded; her bottom plates were ruptured, and she suffered a wobbly drive shaft and a ruptured fire main. After temporary repairs at Funafuti, she sailed for Pearl Harbor on the second anniversary of the attack that brought America to war.

There were a couple of enemy planes sighted by the Southern Attack Force and at least one submarine scare, but nothing very serious had happened until two hours before D-day: the destroyer *Ringgold* and the cruiser *Santa Fe*, pushing along ahead of the main body of Task Force 53, noted a blip on the radar screen moving south at twenty knots. When word was flashed to Adm. Harry Hill, he had to make a difficult decision. The big U.S. submarine *Nautilus*, which had done such excellent reconnaissance on Tarawa, was known to be in the area. But *Nautilus* had been reported as moving westward to look for a downed flyer. Hill further assumed that *Nautilus* would submerge if she encountered friendly forces. Admiral Hill could not take the chance of the contact being an enemy patrol boat, and he gave the order to open fire.

The contact *was Nautilus*. And she did not submerge because she was near a dangerous reef. The first salvo from *Ringgold* was an example of very fine or (very lucky) shooting, a five-inch shell passed through the submarine's conning tower, rupturing a valve. Fortunately, the shell did not explode. Commander Irwin quickly decided that *Nautilus* had less to fear from the reef than from the American destroyers, and he submerged. Fortunately, his ship was not depth-charged, and although it was touch and go for about two hours, *Nautilus*'s crew repaired the damage, and she returned to her duties.

Such stories partially relieved the tension on the bridge of *Maryland,* but the relief was only temporary. At noon on D+1, Admiral Hill and Gen. Julian Smith read the latest message from Colonel Shoup's command post on Betio and, for the thousandth time, asked themselves the question: "Where is the Japanese Fleet?"

9

BEACHES—GREEN
AND BLACK

During the morning of D+1, carrier-based aircraft strafed and bombed the area south of the main airstrip on Betio. Early that afternoon what was left of the marines who had landed on Beach Red 2 the day before crossed the main runway and found the Japanese fortifications on the south shore immediately in front of them completely deserted. There were, however, still occupied Japanese positions to either side of them along the south shore.

The situation in the triangle formed by the taxiways and the main airstrip remained obscure. On Colonel Shoup's orders Lieutenant Colonel Jordan moved his command post across to the south side of the island to take control of the troops there. Jordan reached the south shore at 1600.

The four infantry companies of the Second Battalion, Second Marines that had reached the south shore included about half of an original complement of over 400. The rest were dead or scattered about the island. A regimental weapons unit and a machine-gun platoon were also ensconced on the southern coast of Betio Island. None of the men had food or water, and their ammunition supply was perilously low. Some of the company commanders had begun improvising. Small parties of men were given the job of retrieving and repairing rifles and salvaging ammunition from the cartridge belts of dead marines.

Before Colonel Jordan reached the south beach the defenders hurled a strong counterattack against the Marine position and caused heavy casualties. When Jordan arrived he had a telephone wire laid to connect his units with Colonel Shoup's command post. This gave him, among other things, the capability of calling in naval gun fire in the event of another counterattack.

Jordan's orders were to attack to the east with the aim of linking up with Major Crowe's men on Beach Red 3. Jordan and his company commanders agreed that it was impossible to attack due to the shortage of ammunition and the strength of the Japanese force opposing them. They would be fortunate if they could even repel additional counterattacks. Colonel Shoup, when informed of the situation, agreed that the attack should be postponed until the following morning, and he sent amtracs across the island carrying food, water, and ammunition. On their return trip the tractors brought out the wounded.

At 1800 Maj. Wood Kyle joined Lieutenant Colonel Jordan in the command post on the south coast and, since most of the troops in the area were Kyle's men, Jordan turned them over to him.

About the time Kyle took command, communication with Colonel Shoup's command post was lost. The telephone line had been cut, and as usual, none of the radios worked. When Jordan left to report to Shoup he took two wiremen with him and worked his way back to the command post laying new wire to restore communications.

Major Crowe's Second Battalion, Eighth Marines made little progress during the second day of battle, although not for want of trying. They were still threatened by a counterattack from the east (their left flank), and they had no contact with the marines on their right as D+1 drew to a close. In the late afternoon of D+1 a destroyer fired about eighty rounds of five-inch shells at the bombproof central blockhouse that Admiral Shibasaki had built after the September bombing raids. The shells simply buried themselves in the sand and coconut logs surrounding the structure and did little damage to the reinforced concrete walls.

In the late afternoon of D+1, Robert Sherrod and three of his fellow correspondents were near Major Crowe's command post on Beach Red 3. A grimy marine beside them mused: "I wonder what our transport did with those sixteen hundred pints of ice cream that was to be sent ashore yesterday after the battle was over."

Shortly after 1300 on D+1, a message reached Gen. Julian Smith aboard *Maryland* that Japanese troops were trying to cross the partially submerged sandbar that led to Bairiki, the next island in the atoll east of Betio. General Smith ordered naval gunfire onto the eastern end of Betio and he directed Col. Maurice Holmes, commanding the Sixth Marines who had been held in Corps reserve up to that time, to send one of his landing teams to Bairiki to prevent Japanese troops from leaving Betio. Earlier, Lt. Col. Raymond L. Murray had been told to land his battalion (Second Battalion, Sixth Marines) on Green Beach, following the First Battalion. Murray's men had only just gotten into their boats when they were redirected to Bairiki instead.

At 1408, orders came from division headquarters on *Maryland* that a company of light tanks (Company B, Second Tank Battalion) under Capt. Frank R. Stewart, Jr. was to land on Beach Green as well. The southern end of the beach was littered with obstacles and studded with antiboat mines set ten to fifteen feet apart, so that landing had to be made on the northern end. Unfortunately, the tanks of the three platoons making up the company were loaded in the bottoms of three different ships. Before they could be unloaded all the material stored above them had to be moved. Several hours were lost before the tanks could be lowered over the sides of the transports into the waiting LCMs. (In some cases the intricate combat loading requirements—essential assault equipment should have been loaded in the top and center of each hold—had been frustrated because the hold volumes calculated from the blueprints of the ships were incorrect; some hull alterations had never been entered on those blueprints.)

The First Battalion, Sixth Marines, commanded by Maj. William K. Jones, were to be the first to land on Green Beach. Their vessels were rubber rafts, but known officially as LCRs (Landing Craft, Rubber). The rafts were towed in by Higgins boats as far as the larger vessels could go, but the marines had to paddle the rest of the way. Outboard motors for the rubber rafts had been tried before and proved unreliable. A little before 1400, Jones received a message from Colonel Shoup that read: "Bring in flamethrowers if possible. We are on the southern part of Red 2 and Red 1 zone. Doing our best."

Colonel Holmes advised Shoup that the battalion would land about 1700—the landing had been originally scheduled for two hours earlier. At that point, the battalion's transport, the USS *Feland*, was close to the beach. Just as the LCRs were being lowered into the water *Feland* was ordered to move to deeper water. It was not clear why, and later *Feland* was ordered to stand in again, but valuable time had been lost. It was 1840 when the men of 1/6 (First Battalion, Sixth Marines) splashed ashore on Green Beach.

One of the amtracs that accompanied Jones's men ashore to serve as a supply vehicle struck a mine, was blown apart, and capsized, killing all but one man aboard. Otherwise the landing was generally uneventful by Betio standards. To Major Jones had fallen the honor of commanding the first fully organized Marine unit to land on Tarawa Atoll.

Jones made contact with Maj. Mike Ryan and made a reconnaissance of the lines prior to the attack that Jones thought he was to make at 2000. In fact, Colonel Shoup had sent a message to *Maryland* asking that Jones only hold a beachhead until morning when the attack could be more safely made. Since Jones's men were supposed to attack through the positions held by Major Ryan's battle-weary troops it was essential that the movement be made in good light; the delayed landing had made that impossible. The message had been sent from Shoup's command post at 1748; it was received by Jones, a little more than half a mile away, one hour and thirty-two minutes later, or just forty minutes before he planned to start his

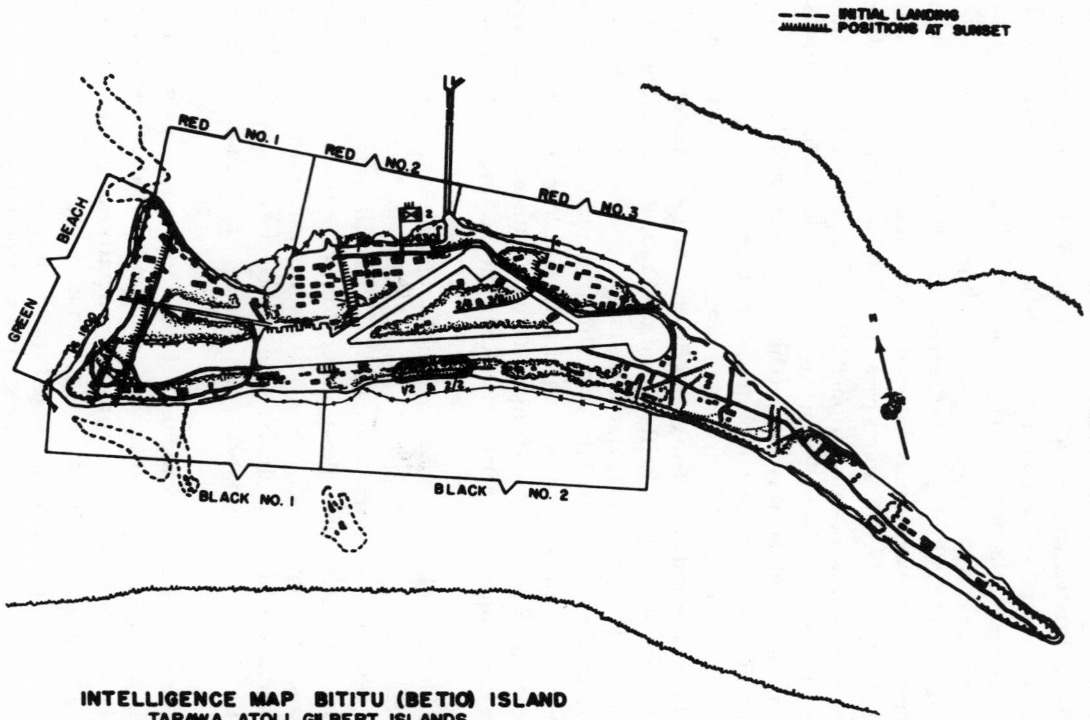

INITIAL LANDINGS
SUBSEQUENT POSITIONS AT SUNSET

NOTE: LINES ARE GENERAL INDICATION ONLY. GAPS WERE COVERED BY SMALL GROUPS AND BY FIRE. SECONDARY LINES WERE ESTABLISHED WHERE POSSIBLE BEHIND FRONT LINES.

RED NO. 3

RED NO. 2

RED NO. 1

BLACK NO. 2

BLACK NO. 1

GREEN BEACH

INTELLIGENCE MAP BITITU (BETIO) ISLAND
TARAWA ATOLL, GILBERT ISLANDS
SITUATION 1800 D+I

500 400 300 200 100 0   1000 YDS

TAKEN FROM 2 D. MAR. DIV
SPECIAL ACTION REPORT

attack. In this case it was "better late than never," and Jones and his men settled down to hold a section of the beach until daylight.

Only one of the three tank platoons was able to negotiate the reef off Green Beach and they landed about the same time as did Jones's men. Because of the difficulties with the reef the other two platoons of tanks sailed around the western end of Betio and landed on Beach Red 2 on the morning of D+2.

Lieutenant Colonel Murray's men (Second Battalion, Sixth Marines), en route to cut off escape from the eastern tip of Betio, encountered machine-gun fire as their boats neared Bairiki, and this fact was reported to division headquarters. The area had been worked over by both naval bombardment and bombing, but when the report of the machine-gun fire came in, the planes that were to support the landing were directed to come in low to find and destroy the machine-gun positions. There was, in fact, only one position; a pillbox containing two guns, fifteen Japanese, and a barrel of gasoline. One of the strafing planes put a .50-caliber slug through the gasoline drum and the guns in the pillbox fell silent in the holocaust that followed.

The marines on Betio had other things to contend with besides hunger, thirst, lack of ammunition, and a determined enemy. One was the heat. Robert Louis Stevenson had written of the Gilbert Islands that they enjoyed "a superb ocean climate, days of blinding sun and bracing wind, nights of a heavenly brightness." The marines took a less romantic view. Nights on Betio were cool thanks to the ever-present trade winds but the days, only a few degrees above the equator, produced what correspondent Richard W. Johnson described as a "kind of skin-cracking heat that was as sharp as a physical blow on the head." The lips of the marines crusted, cracked, and crusted again. The tips of their noses, unprotected from the sun by their helmets, blistered, peeled, then blackened. Under such conditions the men's desire for water was close to overpowering, but for many of them there was no water to be had. The wounded were even more miserable. One of the first symptoms of shock is intense thirst. The injured men wanted water more than anything else in the world, but there was little or none.

Then there was the stink. By late on D+1, it had become nearly unbearable. There had been neither time nor place to bury the dead of either side. Under the tropical sun, the bodies of Japanese and marines fermented, swelled, and burst like overcooked sausages. Intestines sprouted from torn bodies in glistening loops and garlands.

Richard Johnson said:

> The smell was inescapable. It was everywhere and it was not the kind of smell one gets accustomed to. It suffused the marines' hair, their clothing, and seemed to adhere to their bodies. They

smelled it for weeks after the battle, and like all pungent odors, it evoked instant and nightmarish memories.

About 1900 on D+1, Robert Sherrod was back at Colonel Shoup's headquarters watching a doctor working feverishly over a dozen wounded marines lying on the beach. A line strung between a pole and a rifle, bayonet thrust down into the sand, supported four plasma bottles delivering fluid into the arms of four pale marines. The doctor said: "These four will be all right, but there are a lot more up the beach that we probably can't save." He continued:

> This battle has been hell on the medical profession. I've got only three doctors out of the whole regiment. The rest are casualties, or they have been lost or isolated. By now nearly all the (Navy medical) corpsmen have been shot, it seems to me.

Later, Lt. Col. Presley M. Rixey, a blue-eyed Virginian with a moustache, who commanded the artillery attached to Colonel Shoup's regimental combat team, remarked to Sherrod: "You know what, I'll bet these are the heaviest casualties in Marine Corps history."

Amtrac No. 10 was wrecked on the beach, and later that evening, Sherrod and Bill Hipple, a fellow correspondent, began digging their nighttime foxholes alongside it. A marine nearby pointed out that No. 10 came in on the first wave with twenty men in it. All but three were killed by the fire that wrecked the tractor.

Just before dawn on D+2, a Japanese flying boat came over Betio and dropped two sticks of bombs. With fine impartiality, half of them dropped on the marines and the other half on Japanese positions. The bombs killed one marine and wounded another seven or eight.

In spite of the horrors of D+1, the tide of battle was turning. A few minutes after 1700 General Smith received a message from ashore that concluded: "Casualties many, percentage dead not known. Combat efficiency: *we are winning*. Shoup." (Italics added.)

A little later, command of the forces ashore was taken over by Col. Merritt Edson, Gen. Julian Smith's chief of staff, and a nearly exhausted David Shoup was left with only his original command, the Second Marines, to worry about. Nevertheless, both colonels were up all night planning the next day's tactics.

At 1803 the first American jeeps, pockmarked with bullet holes, rolled down the pier towing 37-mm guns. Correspondent Sherrod wrote: "If a sign of certain victory were needed, this is it. Who will carve a monument to the Wheeled Victory of Tarawa?"

10

·Attack!

By making your battle short, you will deprive it of time, so to speak, to rob you of men.

Frederick the Great

Colonel David M. Shoup had commanded the forces ashore on Betio and afloat for two terrible days during which he attempted to coordinate and control the actions of badly disorganized, scattered, and often demoralized units in the face of bitter enemy opposition, primitive communications, and severe supply failures. That he succeeded so well in spite of his wounds was later to be recognized in the award to Colonel Shoup of America's highest decoration, the Congressional Medal of Honor.

That was later. Now, through the night of D+1 and the predawn darkness of D+2, Colonels Shoup and Edson made plans for the daylight attack of the crucial third day of the Betio assault, Monday November 22, 1943.

They asked for naval gunfire on the eastern end of Betio with the fourteen- and sixteen-inch shells to be restricted to an area 500 yards from the nearest Marine positions. At 0700, ships and planes were to bombard the target areas for twenty minutes. This was to be followed by two more twenty-minute bombardments exactly like the first, to begin at 0930 and again at 1030. As the bombardment began Robert Sherrod had a breakfast of hot C rations warmed over a Sterno flame and suddenly remembered that he hadn't eaten for two days. Near the end of the bombardment a destroyer shell found an oil dump in the center of the island; the explosion sent flames soaring above the treetops. The ship poured round after round into the area until a mass of roaring flame and smoke filled the area.

Communications foul-ups continued. The Third Battalion, Sixth Marines, commanded by Lt. Col. Kenneth F. McLeod, had been in Higgins boats since four in the afternoon of D+1; they were bobbing gently near the control vessel at the line of departure in the lagoon. Colonel Shoup's command post was in radio contact with division headquarters on *Maryland*, but neither division headquarters nor Colonel Shoup were in direct contact with McLeod. Nor, for that matter, were they in direct contact with Major Jones and his men (First Battalion, Sixth Marines) on Green Beach. All messages for either unit had to be relayed via the communications center of the Sixth Marine Regiment on the transport that brought them from Makin. It was after dawn when communications were established between Shoup and Jones. (Jones and his men were left temporarily under Shoup's command, although Edson had taken overall command of the Marine forces ashore and in the lagoon.)

Division headquarters finally reached McLeod at 0319 and instructed him to land on Green Beach North at 0800. Forty minutes later, Colonel Edson sent a message to *Maryland* asking to have McLeod's Third Battalion rendezvous off Green Beach *South* at 0800 and await further orders. At 0641, McLeod was ordered to simply wait off Green Beach later that morning and then land wherever he was directed to by Colonel Shoup.

At 0400, Edson and Shoup had completed plans for the attack of D+2. Edson gave verbal orders to Colonels Shoup and Elmer Hall, and Edson sent Maj. R. McC. Tompkins over to Green Beach to deliver his orders in person to Major Jones. On Betio, almost in the middle of the twentieth century, communications were often carried out as they were at the time of Alexander the Great, twenty-four centuries earlier!

The planned attack involved Major Jones's men (1/6) moving through the lines of Major Ryan's weary troops (3/2) to attack eastward along the south coast of Betio until they established contact with the troops of the First and Second battalions, Second Marines under Maj. Wood Kyle, whose efforts of the day before had split the island's defenders into two groups.

An hour after Colonel Edson had sent Major Tompkins to Green Beach with orders for Major Jones he had heard nothing from 1/6. He then sent a message to *Maryland* asking that word be sent to Jones through Sixth Regiment communications telling him of the plans for attack. By then, however, the Sixth Regiment communications center was no longer in touch with its First Battalion.

It was nearly two hours later that Colonel Edson received a message saying that division headquarters aboard *Maryland* was in contact with Major Jones. Half an hour after that, Major Tompkins returned and said that Major Jones had the plan of the attack. His round trip of slightly more than one mile had taken three-and-a-half perilous hours.

At 0815, supported by three tanks operating about fifty yards ahead of the infantry, Jones attacked along the south coast of Betio over a 100-yard front. Jones was to pass through both the Marine lines just east of Green Beach (Major Ryan) and through those of Major Kyle (in about the middle of the island) and then continue the attack eastward toward the tail of the Betio bird as far as possible. In less than three hours, Jones's men had reached Major Kyle's lines on the south (Black) beach at about the center of the airstrip. In the fight along Black Beach 150 mines were deactivated in a stretch of 400 yards. None of the Military Police detachment that did the work had ever deactivated a mine before but their commander, Second Lt. Douglas Key, gave them a demonstration on one mine and told them to go to work.

At daylight, Maj. Lawrence Hays (whose troops had been so horribly mauled in their landing on the previous day), was to attack, with the First Battalion, Eighth Marines, west along the north beach on which the original landings had been made, with the object—often sought but not yet achieved—of wiping out the Japanese strong point on the border between Beaches Red 1 and Red 2.

Colonel Elmer Hall, whose destiny seemed to be leading him to the eastern end of Betio island, whether by land or sea, was to attack in that direction with the Second and Third battalions, Eighth Marines. In Colonel Hall's opinion his men were good for one more attack and then they would have to be relieved. The plans for the assault on D+2, which obviously rested heavily on the relatively fresh men of the Sixth and the Eighth Marines, would give Hall's men this relief after one more heroic effort.

At 0930 that morning an artillery battalion (Second Battalion, Tenth Marines) was ordered into boats with directions to land on Bairiki and set up their batteries to supplement the efforts of the infantry already ashore. One battery landed on Bairiki at 0630 and shortly afterward began firing on the tail of the Betio bird. The second battery, whose unloading from the transports was interrupted by an air alert that caused the transports to move out to sea where they had more room for defensive maneuvers, did not reach Bairiki until noon.

Major Hays's attack against the Japanese strong point on the north beach got under way at 0700 supported by three light tanks. The Japanese defenders had destroyed several tanks by the simple expedient of running up to them and pressing a magnetic mine against the side of the tank. The mine explosion was certain to kill the man who placed it, but it killed the tank and its crew as well. By D+2 the marines had learned about that trick, and riflemen kept a sharp watch on the tanks advancing ahead of them and were constantly ready to shoot any mine-bearing defenders before they reached the valuable tanks, but one of the tanks was still put out of action by a magnetic mine.

Although they were well protected by their accompanying riflemen, the light tanks proved almost useless against the heavy Japanese fortifications. The 37-mm guns they carried were wholly inadequate to the job they faced, and the tanks themselves were too light to crush the enemy emplacements. The Japanese pillboxes were put out of action by riflemen with grenades, flamethrowers, blocks of TNT, and bangalore torpedos (lengths of pipe filled with explosive), in what had become the classical Betio style.

Lieutenant Colonel Jordan, who had complained earlier to correspondent Sherrod because some of the marines held back on the beaches, now said to him: "Tell you something interesting. Once we got these men off the beaches and up front, they were good. They waded into the Japs and proved they could fight just as well as anybody."

Toward noon of D+2 the light tanks were pulled back and their places taken by self-propelled 75-mm guns. But the pillboxes on the north beach were unscathed even by these powerful weapons.

As the afternoon of D+2 wore on, the two companies of Major Hays's battalion that were advancing between the airstrip and the north beach made good progress. Company C, that was attempting to move down the heavily fortified beach itself, could move only very slowly, but the Japanese position was gradually compressed. Late in the afternoon the defenders of the Japanese stronghold tried a modest counterattack against the marines of Company C, but got nowhere. At this time, the western half of Betio was in Marine hands, except for the north beach pocket of resistance that was between Hays's attack from the east and Major Ryan's exhausted men hanging on in the west.

In the morning of D+2 the Seabees (CBs, for Navy Construction Battalion) had begun streaming ashore with their heavy equipment. Now they drove their bulldozers out onto the airstrip and began, in spite of the rifle fire sweeping the open area, to smooth out the shellholes that pocked the runway. Fortunately, the Navy planes had followed orders and done nothing to damage the vital airstrip that was the reason the invasion of Tarawa Atoll was launched. The CBs had other chores as well. One enemy fortification on Betio was constructed of six feet of reinforced concrete overlaid with two feet of sand, then two layers of crisscrossed iron rails, three more feet of sand, two rows of coconut logs, and a final six feet of sand. It had sustained direct hits from 2,000-pound bombs and was unscathed. The CBs finally took it apart layer by layer, drilled a hole into the concrete, and fired a flamethrower through it to take the position out of action.

On Beach Red 3, Major Crowe's Second Battalion, Eighth Marines had also had two days of very hard fighting. Early in the morning of D+2,

Crowe reorganized his men for that day's attack. They still confronted three immense problems. One was a steel pillbox near the Burns-Philp pier to their left. Then there was a substantial coconut-log emplacement from which machine-gun fire periodically swept Company K. Finally, there was a large bombproof shelter inland to the south of the steel pillbox. Each of these three Japanese strongholds was mutually supporting; when one was attacked the marines came under fire from the other two. The plan for D+2 was that the battalion would move against all of these strong points simultaneously.

At 0930 that morning, a mortar round landed directly on top of the coconut-log emplacement, and an ammunition dump inside it exploded. When this happened, Lt. Lou Largey maneuvered the medium tank *Colorado* into a favorable spot west of the steel pillbox and sent several shells into it, putting the pillbox out of the fight. Later, the marines got a good look at the log emplacement. It was made of double thicknesses of eight-inch coconut logs hooked together with steel staples, buttressed by upright logs driven far into the ground, then covered with three feet of shrapnel-absorbing sand. As a Marine engineer remarked to Robert Sherrod: "They've got a good engineer somewhere in this Jap Navy."

The next problem was the bombproof shelter. This stout fortification had fields of fire in all directions and even shells from Marine howitzers and tanks did no significant damage. Assault engineers under Lt. Alexander "Sandy" Bonnyman with flamethrowers and demolitions spent an hour working their way, under the covering fire of riflemen, to the top of the shelter. On the way they exploded TNT charges at the shelter's two entrances and fired flamethrowers into the ports. When the marines reached the top the Japanese in the shelter, under the direct command of Admiral Shibasaki himself, instantly counterattacked but were driven back almost solely by the efforts of Lieutenant Bonnyman who met the attackers first with a flamethrower then with his carbine on full automatic; he drove back those who were not killed. Although repeatedly wounded, Bonnyman fired clip after clip until he finally collapsed. Bonnyman died in this action, but his heroic stand caused the Japanese to begin attempting to evacuate the shelter from the two entrances.

Lieutenant Bonnyman was a lean, handsome graduate of Princeton who, before the war, had owned a copper mine sixty miles from Santa Fe, New Mexico. He had enlisted in the Marines at the age of thirty as a private. Bonnyman was riddled with bullets and fell just an arm's length from the three nearest Japanese who had been killed by his carbine. He was also posthumously awarded a Congressional Medal of Honor.

About the time of Bonnyman's death, a sniper suddenly opened up on Colonel Shoup's command post. The bullets were hitting close to a new ammunition dump near the big pillbox that formed one side of the command post. As Robert Sherrod described it:

Marines who were working on the dump start running. All of us
at headquarters hit the dirt. All except rocklike Dave Shoup. He
stands, fully exposed, arms akimbo, and bellows, "Stop! Goddamn it! What are you running for? Take cover, then move on up
and kill the bastard."

The momentum of Crowe's attack carried his men eastward past the
Japanese buildings until, when they reached the east end of the airfield,
they were endangered by the fire from Major Jones's men advancing east
along the south coast of Betio. Crowe's men withdrew a prudent distance
and spent the remainder of D+2 mopping up enemy positions that they had
bypassed earlier in their advance. At dusk on D+2, Company C of Jones's
battalion took over the front line positions at the eastern end of the airfield
and Crowe's worn-out Company K drew back to form a secondary defense
behind them.

Although some Japanese were found in a crater near Beach Red 3
wearing Marine helmets, jungle dungarees, and boondockers, most of the
Japanese dead were in the standard uniform of the Japanese Special Naval
Landing Forces, a green wool uniform (that must have been nearly
unbearable in the heat of Tarawa Atoll) and wraparound leggings. Many
of the Japanese dead were big men, six feet tall and strongly built, in
keeping with their image as an elite force.

Meanwhile, Lieutenant Colonel McLeod and his men of 3/6 landed on
the northern part of Green Beach, but they had difficulties with the reef and
it was 1100 before the battalion was all ashore. McLeod's men remained in
line until late afternoon when they moved eastward until they were about
600 yards behind Major Jones's First Battalion, where they settled in for the
night.

Also in the morning of D+2, Maj. Gen. Julian Smith decided to move
division command ashore. He and his party (including Brig. Gen. J. L.
Underhill, an observer from Fifth Amphibious Corps, and Brig. Gen.
Thomas Bourke) arrived on Green Beach shortly after McLeod's men.
General Smith inspected the units near Green Beach and then decided that
he could best operate from the already established command post on Beach
Red 2 that had been established by Dave Shoup by the middle of D-day. As
we have seen, the shortest route between two points on Betio was seldom a
straight line. In this case, the move was made by amtrac around the beak of
the Betio bird and into Beach Red 2. The Japanese strong point between
Beaches Red 1 and 2 was still very much in the battle despite the marines'
best efforts to silence it. When General Smith's tractor approached Beach
Red 1, the guns of the strong point opened up on it, wounding the driver
and disabling the vehicle. General Smith and his party transferred to
another tractor and completed the trip to the beach without further incident, arriving there just before 1400. Earlier, Robert Sherrod visited the

command post and saw a line of thirty-one dead marines who had been in the water for two days. "Some were bloated, some have already turned a sickly green. Some have no faces, one's guts are hanging out of its body. The eyeballs of another have turned to a jellied mass after so long in the water."

On the south beach, Major Jones's men had made good progress by the time Jones was called to Colonel Edson's command post to discuss plans for the afternoon. Major F. X. Beamer took command in Jones's absence and moved his men forward. The morning advance of 800 yards had been made against determined opposition, the men were nearly out of water again, and there had been several cases of heat prostration among the marines that morning. Drinking water on Betio was from five-gallon cans filled in New Zealand at least three weeks before. The heat of the South Pacific caused some of the enamel lining to dissolve into the water, or so it was said. Whatever the reason, the water was horrible. The only good water was that which the marines brought ashore in their two canteens that they'd filled before they left the transports, and that was soon gone.

Beamer, in charge of Jones's battalion while Jones was at the meeting with Edson, Julian Smith, and others, tried to replenish his troops' water supply before the afternoon attack. His efforts were largely unsuccessful; most of the men had to continue the attack without water.

By early afternoon, the attack along Black (south) Beach came under heavy-weapon fire from yet another strong concentration of Japanese guns. These positions were composed of guns mounted in steel turrets with 360° traverse. Beamer's forces still had the medium tank *China Gal* and seven light tanks. The light tanks were sent against the emplacement, and the worthlessness of light tanks for such work was again convincingly demonstrated. *China Gal* was finally called in to neutralize the position. A Japanese, naked except for his white cloth G-string, ran out of the pillbox and threw himself under the treads of the tank that was firing 75-mm shells into the fortification. There was a small explosion as the defender's hand grenade went off, but the tread was not blown off and the tank moved forward still firing.

Eventually, *China Gal* took the Japanese position out of action, but it had cost an hour and a half, during which time the advance had been halted. During this interval water was distributed to the entire battalion; Company B, which was to continue the attack, got salt tablets as well. Then Company B moved up through Company A, who had led the attack on the Japanese position, and continued the advance. Company C was sent across the airfield to relieve some of Major Crowe's worn-out men, and the First Battalion, Sixth Marines settled in for the night at the eastern end of the runway. So long as it was light, Company C, on the north side of the airfield, could see their comrades on the south side. Although there was open ground between the two companies it was covered by machine guns.

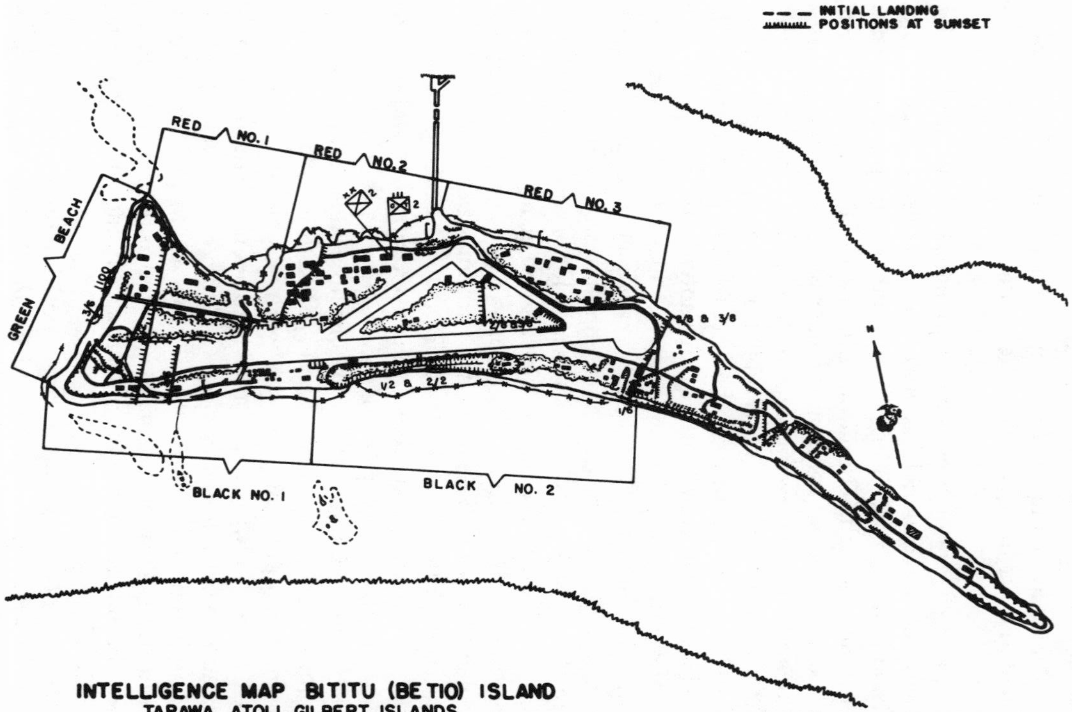

INTELLIGENCE MAP BITITU (BETIO) ISLAND
TARAWA ATOLL, GILBERT ISLANDS

SITUATION 1800 D+2

TAKEN FROM 2D MAR DIV
SPECIAL ACTION REPORT

500 400 300 200 100 0   1000 YDS

--- --- INITIAL LANDING
UUUUUU POSITIONS AT SUNSET

NOTE: LINES ARE GENERAL INDICATION ONLY.
GAPS WERE COVERED BY SMALL GROUPS
AND BY FIRE. SECONDARY LINES WERE
ESTABLISHED WHERE POSSIBLE BEHIND
FRONT LINES.

RED NO. 3
RED NO. 2
RED NO. 1
BLACK NO. 2
BLACK NO. 1
GREEN BEACH

After dark, however, when it was most needed, Company C's radio failed, and they had no further contact with the battalion until the next morning.

As D+2 drew to a close there was an air of foreboding around the division command post on Beach Red 2. The senior officers had discussed the situation there that afternoon. Colonel Edson said: "This is the first beachhead they have really defended. They had no choice but to defend here—they had no interior position to retreat to; it was all exterior." And Colonel Carlson opined: "This was not only worse than Guadalcanal, it was the damndest fight I've seen in thirty years in this business."

Late on D+2 a message came to the command post that confirmed Colonel Carlson's judgment. It was from a shore party who were trying to organize the flow of supplies on the beach and the flow of wounded back to the transports. It said: "Request detail to clear bodies around pier. Hindering shore party operations."

Although the day's advance had been spectacular, especially when measured against the results of the two previous days, it was still maddeningly slow. Julian Smith had committed every man he had. There were no more reserves, and the men who had made the landings on D-day, if not dead or wounded, were completely worn out and could not be considered as fully effective. As another spectacular tropical sunset heralded the end of D+2, General Smith estimated that he had about 7,000 Marine effectives on Betio Island. This was a substantial numerical advantage, but the Japanese defenders had the substantial tactical advantage of being invisible. Many marines at the end of D+2 had been fighting hard all day and had never seen a live Japanese. The defenders fought and died in their fortifications, large and small, and these had to be painstakingly destroyed one by one, at great cost to the marines.

The twin specters of a powerful Japanese counterattack and the appearance of strong Japanese sea and air forces were still very much on the minds of those men on whose shoulders rested the responsibility for the outcome of the battle. Admiral Hill, early on D+1, had received intelligence reports that the Japanese might stage large air attacks through fields on the southern Marshall Islands. It was also reported that Japanese submarines were massing in the area of Tarawa, and that they probably would arrive there on November 23, D+3.

At noon on D+2, the destroyer *Gansevoort* reported a submarine contact west of the transport area. Three hours, and again four hours later, contacts were made but the source could not be located. The destroyer *Frazier* went out to join in the hunt and depth charges were dropped. The enemy submarine was forced to surface, which it did between *Meade* and *Frazier*. The two destroyers immediately opened fire. *Frazier*, leaving nothing to chance, rammed the submarine as well. The submarine was a small vessel the *RC-35*; she yielded three prisoners.

At 1600 on D+2, General Smith sent a message to General Hermle aboard *Maryland* outlining the position ashore in these words:

> Situation not favorable for rapid clean-up of Betio. Heavy casualties among officers makes leadership difficult. Still strong organized resistance area (the map coordinates given were those near the eastern end of the airstrip). Many emplacements intact on the eastern end of the island. . . . In addition, many Japanese strong points to westward of our front lines within our position have not been reduced. Progress slow and extremely costly.

General Hermle's heart must have sunk as he read the next words: "Complete occupation (of Tarawa Atoll) will take at least five days more!" General Hermle knew as well as General Smith that the marines had only a two-day supply of ammunition remaining, and there were twenty-four more islands in the atoll that had to be taken. Bayonets would be of little use against Japanese pillboxes.

11

WHATEVER EXISTS
IS SPIRIT

Japan was the only major country in the world in the twentieth century that combined a modern industrial plant, first-rate armed forces, and social and religious ideas that were those of a far more primitive society.

The slogan *Hakko Ichiu* ("bringing the eight corners of the world under one roof") was the probably mythical utterance of the possibly mythical Emperor Jimmu who came down from the Plains of Heaven in 660 B.C. to rule the Japanese people who were themselves the descendents of lesser gods. On Foundation Day, February 11, schoolboys dressed in samurai costumes celebrated Japan's feudal period when the business of a man was war; this is the day when the Emperor Jimmu descended from Heaven; it is also the day when the Meiji Constitution took effect in 1889. Still further back in the mists of time Japan itself was created by Izanagi and Izanami, a god and goddess who were also brother and sister. They learned to make love by watching a pair of wagtails, and their offspring include the landscape of modern Japan—mountains, waterfalls, and the like—and a host of deities. Izanagi himself gave birth to the sun goddess, Amaterasu, the deity from whom Jimmu and all subsequent emperors were said to be descended. The "circle of the sun" *(hi-no-maru)* adorned the Japanese flag and planes in commemoration of Amaterasu.

Shinto is the indigenous religion of Japan; it had no name for most of the untold centuries of its existence. When Buddhism invaded Japan in the seventh century the word Shinto was invented to distinguish the indigenous religion from the imported one. Before that time what Shinto represented was expressed as *Kami nagara* ("Whatever exists is spirit"). Nature in all its forms, according to the ancient religion, is simply a manifestation of spirit. Death is a transformation from a substantial to an insubstantial form of spirit and is thus of little consequence. Death is analogous to an avalanche or the blocking of a stream by a fallen tree—a rearrangement of the natural world. The Japanese have a sense of dying into the cosmos—a cosmos that encompasses the physical world, all living things, and the souls (*kami*) of the dead. In this cosmos there is neither heaven nor hell, it is a place of harmony. Still, in Japan as elsewhere, death may loom suddenly before one's eyes. As a ninth-century Japanese poet put it: "I knew I had to go this way, but I did not think it was so soon."

Since there are neither deities nor moral teachings in Shinto, the Japanese go to a Shinto shrine in a spirit of reverence but not to worship. What Japanese feel after visiting a Shinto shrine is described by them as a sense of inner renewal, a reenergization. The religion is an amalgam of reverence for both nature and ancestors and particularly for Amaterasu and her descendents. The emperor has the status of a living *kami* (*ikigami*—"a living god or spirit") and is thus someone to whom all Japanese are related. Some Shinto priests and national heroes are also *ikigami*.

So complete was the oneness of the Japanese with nature that a Japanese word had to be invented to express the idea of "nature" as a concept separate from man. This separation, common in Greek thought and given heightened significance in the Christian tradition, never occurred to the Japanese before the Meiji Restoration led to the introduction of Western ideas.

There are approximately 100,000 Shinto shrines in Japan. Every Japanese is a parishioner of one of them and is protected by the regional *kami*. In addition, there are *kami* with special areas of responsibility, such as childbirth, passing examinations, protection against insects, drought, and so on.

Unfortunately, under the Meiji Constitution that came into being in 1889, Shinto became the state religion and the handmaiden of militarism. This corruption, compared to the time scale of more than fifteen centuries of Shinto, was only a temporary aberration, but it still strongly colors Western views of the religion. Under the Meiji Constitution, Shinto and Buddhism, which had largely merged over thirteen centuries, again became two separate religions.

Bushido is a word coined during the Tokugawa Shogunate (the 250 years before the Meiji Restoration) to designate: "the way of the samurai." It referred to the requisite absolute loyalty to the feudal lord (analogous to that of the knights of Europe during its feudal period) and the samurai virtues of willpower, courage, and honor. These virtues are exemplified in the story of the forty-seven *ronin* (unemployed samurai), which is a staple of the Kabuki theater and of Japanese films.

Briefly, the story tells of a provincial official, one Asano, who in 1702 was mortally insulted by Kira, an officer of the shogun. Asano attacked Kira with his dagger but inflicted little injury. The penalty for such an act was death, and Asano committed *hari-kiri* with his own dagger. His samurai, now unemployed, became *ronin*, but they signed an oath of revenge with their leader, Kuranosuke. For a year they were never seen together and Kuranosuke led a life of apparent drunkenness and dissipation.

Then, on December 14, 1703 the *ronin* stormed Kira's mansion, drove off its defenders and demanded that Kira commit *hari-kiri*. He refused, so Kuranosuke beheaded him with Asano's dagger, laid the head on Asano's tomb, and the forty-seven *ronin* then killed themselves and were buried near their former master.

The story has a place of honor in Japanese culture, but it's important to realize that the samurai, who in the sixteenth century and before had spent most of their time fighting in civil wars, became, during the 250 years of peace that characterized the Tokugawa Shogunate, simply armed bureaucrats. Samurai were the elite class who ruled over the other three classes of Tokugawa society: the farmers, the artisans, and the merchants. After the Meiji Restoration of the emperor to primacy, *bushido* again took on the militaristic hue of the pre-Tokugawa samurai and conveniently fused into the new military version of Shinto. *Bushido* made a Japanese proud to serve in the armed forces and ambitious to die for the emperor, for then he would become one of the demigods who hovered over Japan as a mighty spirit army. The *Yasunaki-jinja* shrine, a Shinto sanctuary in Tokyo, is dedicated to soldiers fallen in battle since the Meiji Restoration. The banners display the chrysanthemum, which is the national flower and imperial symbol. *Yasunaki* is the Valhalla of Japan, the place where the spirits of those who died in defense of the country are enshrined. The cartoon characters of Bill Mauldin's Willy and Joe, and the hapless "Sad Sack" would never have arisen in Japan; the army was too sacred to make fun of.

The modern form of *bushido* had other aspects as well. Japan never ratified the Geneva convention since it conflicted with the demands of *bushido*. Every Japanese serviceman knew that should he be hospitalized when a retreat became necessary, he would either be killed by the medical officers or given a hand grenade or rifle to do the job himself.

Dying for the emperor, either by death in battle or by suicide to avoid capture, was expected. As Admiral Yamamoto wrote: "To give up his life for his sovereign and country is the military man's most cherished wish: what difference whether he gives it up at the front or behind the lines?" The Japanese Army manual put it directly: "Bear in mind the fact that to be captured means not only disgracing the Army, but your parents and family will never be able to hold up their heads again. Always save the last round for yourself."

This advice was generally heeded. In most campaigns fewer than one percent of Japanese men were ever captured; some of those were taken because they were surprised, unconscious, or so disabled that they could not take their own lives.

All this makes it easier to understand what happened on Betio Island on the night of D+2.

12

JAPANESE DRINK
MARINE'S BLOOD

The Japanese defenders of Betio Island had forced the marines to pay a heavy price for every yard of bloodstained sand and coral that they had won. They had done so by remaining hidden in the brilliantly designed emplacements and sending withering fire against the marines until each Japanese emplacement was taken out of action. A number of such positions were bypassed in the Marine advance and continued to fire periodically into the rear of the Marine lines.

The strategy of concealment had worked wonderfully well for the dogged defenders of Betio. Why they abandoned it on the night of D+2 will remain forever a mystery. Presumably it was an act of sheer desperation by the exhausted defenders who had abandoned hope of rescue by the ships and planes of their navy comrades, and it was in harmony with the ethics of *bushido*.

Early on the morning of D+2, November 22, 1943, the Japanese radio on Betio sent its last message: "Our weapons have been destroyed and from now on everyone is attempting a final charge. . . . May Japan exist for ten thousand years."

About 1930 some fifty Japanese troops infiltrated between the Marine outposts of the First Battalion, Sixth Marines and opened a gap between Companies A and B. Major Jones sent in his reserves to close the gap and gave orders that the front lines be reorganized and better consolidated. The Japanese counterattack was repulsed after an hour of fighting, largely carried out by the marines with bayonets and hand grenades. They had learned on Guadalcanal not to respond to every probing night attack with automatic-weapons fire because to do so revealed the position of their front lines to the enemy. Once the Japanese counterattack had been turned back, a company of Major Kyle's First Battalion, Second Marines was placed some 100 yards behind the front line to form a second line.

The Japanese attack was probably supposed to reveal the location of the Marine positions in preparation for a much larger attack that would immediately follow. It did not follow immediately because of the marines' restraint in the use of automatic weapons and because of the vicious Marine artillery crossfire that was called down in front of Companies A and B, and which landed only seventy-five yards from the Marine positions. Major Jones had hoped that this fire would catch the main Japanese attack as it moved against the Marine positions. This didn't happen because the barrage was so intense that the island's defenders were unable even to begin their attack in the face of it.

But the Japanese were still determined to carry out a night counterattack. An hour before midnight they tried again with two separate groups of fifty men each who were sent out in front of the two Marine companies. Some of the Japanese simply moved about in the dark, called out to the marines in their positions, while throwing hand grenades and firing rifles. This, again, was an attempt to determine the precise location of the Marine lines, and this effort was more successful because B Company had to resort to machine guns and 60-mm mortars to repulse the attack.

Between the two attacks one of the two medium tanks still in the battle brought up water, small-arms ammunition, and hand grenades to a dump just behind Company A's lines, and Major Jones asked for, and received, naval gunfire on the eastern end of the island to break up any attacking forces that the enemy might be massing there.

At 0300 the defenders began to fire heavy and light machine guns into the Marine lines from weapons set up in some wrecked trucks about fifty yards in front of the Marine positions. Some of the Japanese positions were destroyed by Marine heavy machine-gun fire, three other enemy guns were destroyed by sergeants and corporals who crawled out to them with hand grenades.

Suddenly 300 men threw themselves against the lines held by Company B and the right front of Company A screaming "Marine, you die!" and "Japanese drink marine's blood." Lieutenant Thomas, acting commander of B Company, telephoned Major Jones to report that: "We are killing them as fast as they come at us, but we can't hold out much longer; we need reinforcements." Jones's reply offered cold comfort on a suddenly hot morning. "We haven't got them. . . . You've got to hold."

Sixty minutes later, the counterattack had failed. More than 200 Japanese dead lay in front of the Marine lines. In the area pounded by Marine artillery there were some 125 enemy dead. East of that, fire from the destroyers *Schroeder*, and later *Sigsbee*, kept reinforcements from being organized to assist the Japanese counterattack. Jones's men had taken 173 casualties. Just before the Japanese counterattack that morning, four enemy planes arrived to bomb the island, but they accomplished very little.

The First Battalion, Sixth Marines had had a hard night, and Col. Maurice Holmes, commanding the Sixth Marines, ordered up the Third Battalion to relieve the First Battalion at daylight and continue the attack eastward at 0800.

U.S. carrier planes came in to bomb and strafe the eastern end of the island between 0700 and 0730. Marine artillery took over for fifteen minutes after that, and naval gunfire provided the final fifteen minutes of softening for the remaining defenders on the eastern end of the island, the long tail of the Betio bird.

Substantially more than a mile, 2000 yards, of Betio Island remained in Japanese hands on the morning of D+3. The area had been heavily bombarded on D-day and each day since. In places, rows of contiguous shellholes marched from the Marine lines to the shallow water at the very tip of the Betio bird's tail. In spite of this pasting, the area still contained dugouts, block houses, log and dirt emplacements, and rifle pits fully functional and manned by defenders who, dazed, hopeless, and beyond exhaustion, clearly hoped to take as many marines as possible with them on their journey to the warriors' heaven. But the defenders' mutually supporting positions were not manned by the Japanese with their customary enthusiasm, and this made the marines' job easier. This may have been because the defenders had been fighting hard for three days against marines who had had the comparative luxury of at least some replacements in the front lines. The Japanese may have been totally exhausted and discouraged by then; they may also have been very low on ammunition.

Plans for the Marine attack had been made at General Smith's command post in a meeting of his top officers; the conference began at almost the same time as the first small Japanese counterattack. The Sixth Marines, with all available tanks, were to continue toward the eastern tip of the island.

On the morning of November 23 (D+3), about 500 Japanese still remained on the tail of the Betio bird, along with those still holed up in other positions elsewhere on the island. There were also about 160 Japanese on Buariki with rifles, hand grenades, at least ten machine guns, and two knee mortars. (The knee mortar was actually a spring-actuated grenade launcher. Because of its curved base, the marines thought the Japanese braced the mortar on their knees for firing, but they didn't.) Eight Japanese had escaped to tiny Lone Tree Islet at the farthest end of the lagoon from Betio.

The Second Marine Regiment (The Second Marines) was to continue mopping-up operations that were to be particularly directed toward the seemingly indestructible strong point between Beaches Red 1 and Red 2.

The Eighth Marines, less one battalion that had been detached to help out the Second Marines, was to prepare to move to the neighboring island of Bairiki when boats were available and begin the neutralization of any Japanese troops left on the other islands of Tarawa Atoll.

The Japanese strong point between Beaches Red 1 and 2 had taken countless marine lives. It now received the undivided attention of two Marine battalions. It took two hours to encircle the enemy pocket. Two 75-mm self-propelled guns and a platoon of infantry led by Maj. Hewitt D. Adams even went out on the hated reef and attacked the Japanese emplacement from close range. From the east, all three companies of Maj. Lawrence Hays's First Battalion, Eighth Marines struck with other 75-mm self-propelled guns, flamethrowers, and demolition teams. On the west side, Maj. John Schoettel's Third Battalion, Second Marines spread out until they contacted the men on the reef and some of Hays's men near the airstrip. (It had taken Major Schoettel until D+2 to rejoin his battalion.) Then the three groups drew the now joined circle of marines in on the fortified positions. The enemy position was vulnerable from its rear, and by 1300 the fortifications had been reduced, although blasting and burning of its various components went on for the rest of the day.

When the attack toward the eastern end of the island began at 0800, Lieutenant Colonel McLeod took over while Jones's tired men, after handing over to McLeod's men all their available tanks and flamethrowers, moved back into secondary reserve. With Colonel McLeod and his men of 3/6 went the two remaining functional Sherman tanks, *Colorado* and *China Gal*, along with seven light tanks.

The advance went smoothly for some 350 yards with I Company on the left or north side, its left flank on Beach Red 3, and L Company on the right, its right flank on the heavily defended south (Black) beach of the island. Then I Company hit a formidable obstacle, another series of mutually supporting bombproof shelters laid out with the designer's customary skill and now inhabited by most of the surviving defenders who had gathered for one last effort before the hoped-for arrival of the *rengo kantai* that would turn the tide against the marines.

I Company and Lt. Lou Largey with the crew of *Colorado* remained behind to deal with the strong point. At the same time Colonel McLeod directed L Company to continue along the south shore and, after it was out of range of the massed Japanese weapons, to spread out across the whole of Betio Island, there only about 200 yards wide.

The marines of I Company moved against the fortified positions with flamethrowers and rifles. All at once the defenders in the biggest blockhouse erupted from it into the narrow exit channel. An infantry spotter bloodied his knuckles rapping frantically on *Colorado*'s armored side. Lou Largey responded by swinging the tank around, depressing his .75-mm gun barrel, and firing point blank into the mass of men packed in the exit channel. There was not enough left of the Japanese troops in the channel to count, but Largey figured he got fifty to seventy-five with his single shot. Whatever the number, that shot put an end to resistance in the Japanese strong point and I Company could move on eastward.

Company L moved on toward the tip of the bird's tail while I Company was busy with the strong point. *China Gal* rumbled back and forth across the narrowing island to wherever her armored firepower was needed. The seven light tanks likewise went wherever their popgun-sized weapons could be effectively employed.

About noon a Navy Hellcat fighter landed on the airfield on Betio Island. It was the first of many American planes to touch down on this hard-won "unsinkable aircraft carrier" that would supply vital support for the Marshall Islands invasion planned for thirty-eight days hence. The main runway was concrete and was in almost perfect condition. The shorter runways, of gravel, were also in good shape. There were numerous Japanese planes along the runways, both Zero fighters and twin-engined bombers. A nearby Japanese truck had four different brands of tires attesting to past Japanese successes: Dunlop, Bridgestone, Yokohama, and Firestone. A black Japanese Navy sedan had blackout oilcloths over the headlights. The hole in the oilcloths was the shape of an anchor that, in Robert Sherrod's phrase: "makes the headlights look like a Hallowe'en pumpkin." The airfield, won at such terrible cost, would soon be officially named Hawkins Field in honor of the gangling, young lieutenant whose courage and endurance so inspired his fellow marines on Betio.

At about 1300 on D+3, a tired, sweaty marine stepped into the tepid water washing over the long sand spit on the eastern end of Betio Island and washed his grimy face in the warm salt water. A few minutes later, Lt. Gen. Julian Smith announced that Betio was officially "secured." Secured has several meanings in Navy and Marine jargon. In this case, it meant that organized resistance on Betio no longer existed. It did not meat that life on Betio had suddenly become secure; a number of marines were killed by snipers for several days afterward, but the terrible battle for Betio was officially at an end. It had lasted for seventy-five hours and forty-two minutes from the time that the first marines had hit the Betio beach.

There were twenty-four more islands in Tarawa Atoll, and there might be Japanese troops on any or all of them. There was, moreover, the threat of a counterlanding by fresh Japanese troops supported by sea and air forces.

The first problem was started on its way to solution late in the afternoon when Col. Elmer Hall moved the Eighth Marine Regiment, minus Hays's battalion, by boat from Betio to Bairiki to spend the night and secure that approach from counterattack. Late the next afternoon, Lt. Col. Raymond Murray learned that he and his men (2/6) who, because of a shortage of boats had not arrived in Betio from Bairiki in time to take much part in the final attack on D+3, were to set off in the morning to secure the remaining islands of Tarawa Atoll for the United States.

The more pressing problem, that of protecting against a possible coun-

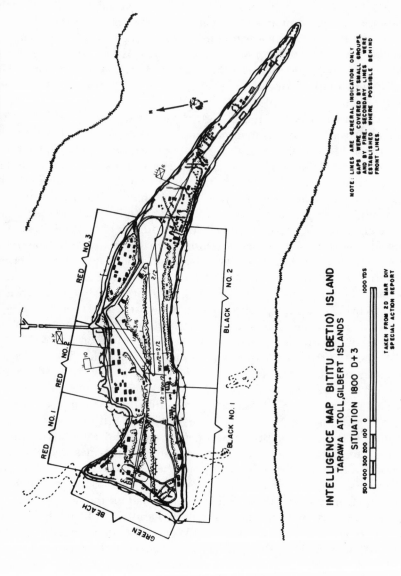

POSITIONS AT SUNSET

NOTE: LINES ARE GENERAL INDICATION ONLY. GAPS WERE COVERED BY SMALL GROUPS AND BY FIRE. SECONDARY LINES WERE ESTABLISHED WHERE POSSIBLE BEHIND FRONT LINES.

INTELLIGENCE MAP BITITU (BETIO) ISLAND
TARAWA ATOLL, GILBERT ISLANDS
SITUATION 1800 D+3

500 400 300 200 100 0   1000 YDS

TAKEN FROM 2D MAR DIV
SPECIAL ACTION REPORT

terlanding on Betio, was taken care of by moving men and weapons to the perimeter of the island where they had good fields of fire out over the water, while the artillery and mobile reserves were kept on the interior of the island ready to move against any landing force should it appear.

Simultaneously, during the afternoon of D+3, the marines took up defensive positions, began to bury Japanese and American dead, and destroyed or buried pillboxes that still meanced the passing marines. All the men, with the possible exception of Lieutenant Colonel Murray's men who had had the easiest time of it so far and were itching to start on their own campaign along the string of islands in the atoll, were dead tired and hoping for a quiet night as a reward for their Herculean labors. It was not to be. At 1800, a marine tossed a thermite (incendiary) grenade into what he thought was an enemy pillbox. It was, instead, the magazine for a five-inch gun. Shells in the magazine continued to explode and rain down shrapnel onto the weary marines all night long. To add insult to injury, a few of the island's diehard defenders took advantage of the fireworks to come out of hiding and attack the marines in the dark. Two enlisted men were fatally bayoneted in their foxholes and a Marine intelligence officer was killed as were fourteen more Japanese.

Major Howard J. Rice, at twenty-five, was probably the youngest battalion commander in the Marine Corps since he had assumed command of 2/2 after Colonel Amey's death on D-day. His battalion adjutant, Lt. Albert Borek, talked to Robert Sherrod as they took their ease in a tank trap on the south shore on the night of D+3. Lieutenant Borek said: "I'm afraid to tell you what the battalion casualties were. The best count I can get is 309 men left out of 750 who landed. There are fifteen officers left out of thirty-nine."

On the morning of November 24 transports had moved into the lagoon and the Second and Eighth Marines, one regiment from Betio and one from Bairiki, left Tarawa Atoll for the long voyage to the next station, 2,000 miles away in Hawaii.

On that same day, there was a twin flag-raising ceremony on Betio where the Stars and Stripes were raised on one denuded palm tree while the Union Jack was raised on another. The ceremony was delayed while a search was made for a British flag. Finally, Maj. Frank L. G. Holland, the former Gilbert Island schoolmaster who had correctly predicted the murderously anomalous tides in Betio's lagoon, and who had come with the invasion forces as an advisor and as a representative of His Majesty's government, was able to produce a small Union Jack for the occasion.

Later that day, correspondent Sherrod took a walking tour near Beach Red 1 and the throat of the Betio bird, an area in which an estimated 250 marines had been killed. "Here amtrac No. 15—name: 'Worried Mind'—is jammed against the seawall. Inside are six dead marines, next to it are three more. Two more lie impaled on the barbed wire next to the twenty-eight seater Jap privy over the water. Their clothing ties them to the wire. They float at anchor."

Gene Seng and Charlie Montague, aged twenty-one, had been childhood friends. They had gone to school together. On February 3, 1942 they had volunteered for the Marines together. On November 20, 1943 they died together on Betio. Montague's body was found on the beach near amtrac No. 15. Both men had been in D Company of the Eighteenth Marines, an engineer regiment.

Sherrod continued along the west beach where Japanese pillboxes were only ten feet apart. Along the road from the airfield were one-man sniper pits—gasoline drums sunk into the ground with a lid for a cover. "Outside the gun emplacement (a 5.5-inch gun on the forehead of the Betio bird) a dog, suffering from severe shell shock, wanders drunkenly. When some marines whistle and call him he trembles and tries to run, and falls."

The march up the islands of Tarawa Atoll began on Thanksgiving Day, November 25, 1943. The marines marched all day, accompanied by a crowd of Gilbertese natives who wanted to help the marines carry their gear, show them the best places to ford between the islands, and generally to be as helpful as possible. The marines were delighted, especially since the baneful missionary influence had not yet persuaded the young women of the smaller islands that any clothing other than a grass skirt was needed in that oppressive climate.

At night the marines and the natives bivouacked a discreet distance apart and amused each other with songs in their respective languages. A Tarawan named Tutu, who had studied at the medical college of Fiji and spoke excellent English, interpreted for Colonel Murray and kept his exuberant countrymen (and women) under control. On Thanksgiving Day the marines had gotten into trouble fording a channel between two islands when the tide rose suddenly. Mr. Tutu swam across with a few natives and returned with three canoes that were used to ferry the marines across the channel.

That same day, Maj. Gen. Holland Smith made an inspection tour of Betio in the company of Maj. Gen. Julian Smith. Impressed by the Japanese defenses, Holland Smith remarked to Robert Sherrod:

> These Japanese were masters of defensive construction. The Germans never built anything like this in France. No wonder those bastards were sitting back here laughing at us! They never dreamed the Marines could take this island, and they were laughing at what would happen to us when we tried.

Three marines were killed by Japanese snipers on the western end of the island shortly after the Generals Smith had passed that point.

The first day's march of Colonel Murray and his men did not uncover any of Tarawa's defenders. By midafternoon of the second day the marines reached the last island of the atoll, Buariki, where any surviving Japanese had to be, unless they had somehow been rescued. Lieutenant Colonel Murray sent E Company ahead to reconnoiter, and at sunset, they encountered a Japanese patrol. Two marines were wounded and two Japanese died in the sudden little firefight, and Murray and his men dug in for a possible night attack. The defenders spoiled the marines' sleep by occasional sniping throughout the night, but there was no counterattack.

The next day 2/6 made up for the "good duty" they had had on Betio. The Japanese were everywhere in thick jungle reminiscent of Guadalcanal, and the only plan the marines had was to get them out of there. The marines advanced, with E and G companies in the van and F Company in reserve. Company E got badly cut up, and the battle against the difficult terrain and the desperate enemy lasted all day. During the battle at the end of Buariki, the Gilbertese women made palm-frond pillows for the wounded marines, fanned away flies, brought fresh water, and made themselves generally useful, while Mr. Tutu showed that he knew how to handle surgical instruments.

By nightfall, the battle was over. The last pocket of Japanese resistance on Tarawa Atoll had been obliterated; 175 Japanese lay dead in the jungle, and the Second Battalion, Sixth Marines had 91 casualties. Tarawa Atoll was now secured.

13

AFTERMATH

Ye lust, and have not;
ye kill, and desire to have,
and cannot obtain;
ye fight and war,
yet ye have not.

James 4:1

The battle for Tarawa Atoll was over, militarily. For the widows and orphans in Japan and the United States it would not be over for a long time, nor would it for those maimed in battle who would often be reminded of Tarawa over weeks, or months, or years of pain as their wounds healed and they were returned either to the vigorous good health they had previously enjoyed or to a lifelong struggle against their disabilities. For the eighteen-year-old, now blind, legless, or hideously burned, the battle was only beginning.

The Japanese lost 4,690 men on Tarawa; only 17 were captured, along with 129 Korean laborers. Of the total Japanese garrison, 2,619 were members of the Special Naval Landing Forces.

The U.S. forces lost 57 Marine and 2 Navy officers killed, along with 898 Marine and 27 Navy enlisted men (the Navy men were medical corpsmen or Seabees). In addition 88 Marine and 2 Navy officers were wounded, as were 2,023 Marine and 49 Navy enlisted men. Eighty-eight enlisted marines were missing. One officer and fourteen enlisted men were evacuated because of combat fatigue. The Second Marine Division had had only 263 men killed in six months on Guadalcanal.

About half the dead were killed in the water, nearly all of the wounded were hit on shore.

Some units had very high casualties. Of the Second and Eighth Marine regiments, thirty-five percent were killed, wounded, or missing; more than one in three. Of the men who carried flamethrowers, two-thirds were killed. (Subsequent to Tarawa, all marines were trained in the use of flamethrowers and demolitions, training previously only given to engineers.) The amtrac battalion suffered 325 casualties out of a prebattle strength of 661. Of the 125 amtracs, 35 sank at sea, 26 sank on the reef, 9 burned on the beach when their gasoline tanks were set on fire, and 2 were blown up by mines. Only fifty-three ever got to the beach, and a third of those were destroyed before the battle was over.

Another of several tactical and strategic firsts for Operation Galvanic occurred on D+6, after Tarawa Atoll was secured, when the Japanese launched a night attack on Admiral Radford's Northern Carrier Group. The admiral had organized a radar-equipped night combat air patrol to break the Japanese monopoly on night air strikes. The result was the first nighttime air battle in carrier history. The Japanese were so surprised that they began shooting down each other and not a single American ship was hit. The only tragedy marring this achievement was that Lt. Comdr. E. H. "Butch" O'Hare, who had won a Congressional Medal of Honor for shooting down five Japanese bombers off Bougainville and saving *Lexington* from certain destruction was lost in the nighttime melee; Chicago's airport was named after him in memoriam. The Japanese Imperial Headquarters referred to this action as "the Air Battle of the Gilberts" and claimed that two big carriers and two cruisers were sunk and another battleship or cruiser was "set ablaze."

Also, at Makin, during that portion of Operation Galvanic, a Japanese submarine sank the escort carrier *Liscombe Bay* and escaped untouched. Six hundred sixty-four men were lost.

The casualties horrified the American public, who had not been prepared for the cost of assaulting a heavily fortified beach. Guadalcanal, after six months, had claimed 4,123 American lives. To have lost nearly 1,000 men in seventy-six hours struck the American man in the street as obscene. He would soon learn that this kind of warfare was costly of young lives, torn flesh, and spilled blood. On Iwo Jima the Marines lost 25,851 men in less than four weeks. On Okinawa, 49,151 men died in eighty-two days. If the six Marine divisions scheduled to invade Japan on November 1, 1945 had had to carry out that assignment, the casualties—both Japanese and American—would have been the highest the world had ever seen, and Japan would have been reduced to a smoking ruin running blood.

But the butcher's bill at Tarawa could have been much higher if the situation had been only slightly different. The defenses of Betio Island, formidable though they were, were focused exclusively on throwing invaders back into the sea before they were able to claw out a toehold on the beach. Defenses inland were much less formidable than they might have been. This may have been because Admiral Shibasaki simply did not have either the time or the material to improve them; this explanation is made more probable by the fact that the beach defenses were not yet complete at the time of the landing. Or it may have been the result of doctrinal rigidity keyed on defense at the water's edge.

As Japanese Imperial Headquarters later explained: "The beaches where the enemy landed were the points where both our fortified positions lacked equipment and our troop disposition was weak, and especially points where there were no antitank obstacles." Invasion of the south beach, where the defenses were completely developed, would have been much more costly and would have been further complicated by heavy surf that the lagoon side did not have.

It would have been comparatively simple to erect inland fortifications that would have made crossing the airstrip, for example, extremely costly, but such positions were only hastily erected after the marines were ashore. Similarly, the large structures that were ultimately used as defensive positions by the Japanese were barracks and storage areas and were not designed as fortifications. They often lacked sufficient gun ports to give overlapping fields of fire, for example, and frequently had blind sides that were vulnerable to attack.

One bit of information that would have comforted the marines huddled on the beach through the night of D-day was that, while the Japanese Army had mortar platoons, their navy did not. The lack of heavy mortars on the island was a gross error on the part of the defenders, an error to which many marines owed their lives.

The air raids on November 18-19 that preceded the marines' landings knocked out two of the four eight-inch coast-defense guns from Singapore, and three of the seven Japanese tanks that had been mobile were damaged then. But perhaps the most important effect that these raids had was that they seriously depleted the supply of ammunition available to the defenders of Betio. By dawn of D-day they had only 4,800 rounds of 75-mm and 127-mm antiaircraft ammunition (for their dual purpose guns) and only 15,000 rounds of 13-mm machine-gun ammunition. This fact had been picked up by the Navy's Combat Intelligence Unit at Pearl Harbor but was not decoded in time to be relayed to the Southern Attack Force.

The preinvasion naval bombardment did not knock out the strongest Japanese pillboxes, but it did demolish most of the aboveground buildings, that were not specially strengthened, and it silenced most of the big guns on Betio. Colonel Evans Carlson, highly experienced in such matters, said that not more than five guns bigger than an automatic rifle were firing at the amtracs when he came ashore about 1000 on D-day. There had been forty-five guns that size on the south side of the island alone before the naval bombardment, although some of them may have been taken out of action by the carrier-aircraft raids of the preceding two days. The most important aspect of the air raids and the D-day bombardment may have been that they killed about forty percent of the island's defenders before the first amtracs ground ashore on Red Beach 1.

The naval bombardment also destroyed the Japanese communications so that defensive efforts could not be effectively coordinated, and the defenders did not make efficient use of runners—in part, perhaps, because of lack of training in this type of communications by the Japanese Navy units—and in part because the bombardment made it impossible for runners to get through. As Colonel Shoup's Japanese language officer, Capt. Eugene P. Boardman, put it:

> Strangely enough, the naval troops on Tarawa used no message blanks. In previous operations, as on Guadalcanal, field message blanks constituted a prominent part of the "take" of captured Japanese documents. This total absence of message blanks surprised us. It showed, I believe, the complete doctrinal reliances of the defenders of Betio upon wire communication and indicated a lack of training in using runners. The effectiveness of the preliminary bombardment in breaking up the Japanese wire communication system was probably all the more fateful on this account.

It is entirely possible that the lack of Japanese communications prevented any significant counterattack on the Marine lines on the marines' first night ashore.

Although the naval bombardment had not been as effective as Admiral Kingman and his colleagues hoped it would be, it was not as ineffectual as it has sometimes been made to sound. As Gen. Holland M. Smith, in his action report on Galvanic wrote: "The naval bombardment prior to the actual landing . . . did not prevent enemy resistance. This does not mean that it was not effective, for without naval gunfire, the landing could not have been made."

Immediately after Tarawa Atoll was secured, the defenses of Betio were duplicated on the naval gunnery range on Kahoolawe Island in Hawaii and a systematic study made of how to demolish such structures. After the invasion it was also clear that the mean center of impact of the naval projectiles had been inland on Betio rather than along the beaches. Still the first three waves of marines got ashore nearly intact before the defenders recovered from the bombardment sufficiently to contest the landing that they had been expecting.

Special Duty Ensign Kiyoshi Ohta (the only Japanese Navy officer captured on Betio) explained:

> We expected the American assault at high tide and we made the necessary preparation accordingly. We knew the Americans would suffer the least casualties if they landed on high tide.
>
> I think that due to the enormous bombardment from the air and from the naval vessels the Americans thought that there would be no Japanese; at least, if there were, they would all be wounded or killed soldiers by this time. We took them by surprise and there was a great confusion among the enemy at that time.

It was a statement with which few of the marines could disagree.

Another important contribution to the successful invasion of Tarawa Atoll was the debilitated condition of the air arm of the Imperial Combined Fleet and the consistent mishandling of the fleet by Admiral Koga.

On the morning of D-2, November 18, 1943, the Northern (Makin) Attack Force was sighted by Lt. Kichi Yoshuyo. He reported: "Fleet sighted. Several carriers and other types too numerous to mention. . . ." The warning had little effect.

Admiral Koga had previously decided that the U.S. Pacific Fleet was getting ready to attack Wake Island. In order to be in a good position for the decisive fleet action that naval commanders on both sides constantly sought, he sailed the Combined Fleet to Eniwetok in the Marshall Islands, 400 miles northwest of Kwajalein. He dallied there for a week, then decided that the Wake threat was a false alarm and sailed back to Truk on October 24 as the marines of the Second Marine Division were beginning to notice that Wellington Harbor was filling up with the transports that would take them to Tarawa Atoll.

Admiral Koga then stripped his carriers of all their planes in order to reinforce Rabaul. Then news of the Bougainville landing caused him to shift his ships southward.

A number of vessels that had been held at Truk in accordance with the Z plan were moved to Rabaul to stop the American advance in that direction. Admiral Kurita's heavy cruiser squadron arrived at Rabaul at sunrise on November 5 and began refueling. When the cruisers and oilers were neatly laced together with a tapestry of lines and hoses, planes from *Saratoga* and *Princeton* of Admiral Sherman's force pounced with bombs and torpedos. Seven of the nine cruisers were so badly damaged that they were sent wallowing back to Japan for repairs, and the other two retired to Truk.

The carrier pilots of Admiral Sherman's *Saratoga* and *Princeton* and Admiral Montgomery's *Essex, Bunker Hill,* and *Independence* had been enjoying themselves so much that they returned to Rabaul for an encore a week later. What was left of the Japanese carrier aircraft retired to Truk the next day. In two weeks time, Admiral Koga had lost half his Zero (Zeke) fighters, 85 percent of his Vals (dive-bombers), nine out of ten of his torpedo bombers (Kates), and nearly half of his pilots and aircrewmen. His fleet of aircraft was reduced from 173 planes to 52. Although it was not then appreciated, the back of Japan's awesome naval power had been broken no later than five days after the marines landed on Tarawa Atoll, largely by a series of fifteen naval battles (mostly at night) in the Solomon Islands. Although the Japanese got draws or won ten of the fifteen, the overall result was devastating. Japan could no longer replace lost ships at the necessary rate while a burgeoning stream of new vessels poured from American shipyards and sailed out into the Pacific.

Moreover, while the Japanese won no further naval battles (of ship against ship) after the Battle of Vella Lavella on October 7, 1943, the U.S. Navy won eight. By the beginning of 1944 the Japanese had lost thirty-three ships in eight months, including a battleship, an escort carrier, three light cruisers, and twenty-five of the particularly valuable destroyers, in addition to those ships so seriously damaged that they were effectively removed from combat. The result was that the Japanese sea and air forces were so badly cut up that the Z plan could no longer be considered an effective response to an American thrust into the Gilberts. Others of Koga's ships dashed frantically from island to island in the Central Pacific but nothing was accomplished but the consumption of thousands of gallons of precious fuel oil. When the Northern Attack Force was spotted, Admiral Koga sent troops on the light cruisers *Isuzu* and *Naka* from Kwajalein to reinforce Tarawa Atoll, and Fourth Fleet headquarters was transferred to the Marshalls, better to direct the counterattack. The heavy cruisers *Jumano*, *Chokai*, and *Suzuya* drove at flank speed toward the Gilberts with bones in their teeth and great wakes roiling out astern. But it was too late. Tarawa Atoll had fallen. The troops went to Mili, and the ships dispersed without firing a shot. In sum, the vessels of the fearsome Combined Fleet, thus mangled and mismanaged, were never a threat to the invasion of Tarawa Atoll.

As Vice Adm. Shigeru Fukudome put it when he was interrogated after the war: "Although the Gilberts fight appeared to be the last chance for a decisive fight, the fact that the fleet's air strength had been so badly depleted enabled us to send only very small air support to Tarawa and Makin. The almost complete loss of carrier planes was a mortal blow to the fleet since it would require six months for replacement. . . . In the interim, any fighting with carrier forces was rendered impossible."

Because of the great gulf between the Imperial Army and the navy it was a month after Midway before General Tojo learned the extent of the navy's losses there, despite his position as prime minister and war minister. Thus, it is quite likely that Japanese newspapers were more often than not completely in the dark concerning imperial reverses on the battlefield. In any case, the Japanese accounts of the loss of the Gilberts were remarkably sanguine.

Asahi remarked, on November 24 (D+4) that: "It is clear that the new offensive (against the Gilberts) was launched for other reasons than military strategy. It was a political strategy to divert the eyes and ears of the American people from the great losses incurred at Bougainville. . . . Do not be intoxicated by battle results." That there were great losses as a consequence of the Bougainville invasion was indisputable, but *Asahi* seemed confused as to which side had sustained them. *Yomiuri* took a philosophical view: "As in judo, let the enemy push and push. Then at the end we shall make use of his strength to throw him over."

As we have seen, victory at Tarawa Atoll depended intimately on the close cooperation over vast stretches of the Pacific Ocean among the Army Air Forces, the U.S. Navy, and the Marine Corps. Still, this seventy-six-hour battle was, on its face, only an incident in the four-year-long Pacific war. A few months later the killing ground had moved north and Tarawa Atoll returned to its prewar somnolence.

Yet this brief but violent struggle marked a turning point in the Pacific war. Two major strategic innovations came out of the Second World War, one was long-range strategic bombing, the other was amphibious assault. Although the first played a role at Tarawa, as we have seen, amphibious *assault* against a highly fortified beach (as distinct from amphibious *operations* such as the North African and most of the Normandy landings) was tried for the first time at Tarawa since the Gallipoli fiasco.

It has sometimes been suggested that the invasion of Salerno, which began on September 9, 1943, was the first assault on a heavily fortified beach, rather than the landing on Tarawa more than two months later. These two actions were, however, very dissimilar.

The German Sixteenth Panzer Division (some 45,000 inexperienced men—the division had been decimated at Stalingrad and recently reconstituted) had arrived in Salerno only a few days before the invasion and had the task of defending some twenty miles of curving beach, behind which was a flat plain. The Germans hurriedly constructed six strong points along the beach to harrass invaders. Each of these were manned by an infantry platoon with heavy machine guns, mortars, antitank, and antiaircraft guns, but there was no continuous defensive line along the beaches. And, unlike at Tarawa, the strong points were put out of action early by ground and naval gunfire. There were a few mines on the beaches and a small amount of barbed wire. The Panzer Division had 100 tanks, but communication between them and their headquarters was poor so they were not effectively utilized, and, because of irrigation and drainage canals, walls, and fences, it was bad country for tanks. Also, the tanks were not much used before daylight, two hours after the invasion had begun.

The Allied invasion began on two sets of beaches eight miles apart. The

American beaches in the south were the province of the Army's 36th Division. The three regiments of the overstrength division each contained some 9,000 men all of whom were ashore by the end of D-day. Some parts of the American beaches received very heavy fire, and the first day was one òf casualties and confusion, illuminated by numerous acts of great courage and resourcefulness. In this latter respect the Salerno invasion resembled the Tarawa action. The trouble at Salerno did not come during the amphibious assault, but later, when German reinforcements began to pour into the area to contain the landing. By the end of D-day, however, the 36th Division at Salerno had achieved its objectives at the cost of only 100 dead.

Tarawa remains the first instance of an amphibious assault against a heavily fortified beach since the disaster at Gallipoli.

There were at least a hundred mistakes made at Tarawa, as the Marine Corps was the first to admit, but the correction of these mistakes made possible the landings on Guam, Saipan, Tinian, Peleliu, Iwo Jima, and finally Okinawa—the latter only 500 miles from the Japanese home islands. The Okinawa operation was the longest and bloodiest of all, it consumed eighty-four days and cost over 200,000 American casualties, but it was only possible at all because of the painful lessons learned at Tarawa.

As Gen. Alexander A. Vandegrift later put it:

> Despite its outstanding record as a combat force in the last war, the Marine Corps' far greater contribution to victory was doctrinal, that is, the fact that the basic amphibious doctrines which carried Allied troops over every beachhead of World War II had been largely shaped—often in the face of uninterested or doubting military orthodoxy—by U.S. Marines, and mainly between 1922 and 1935.

This doctrine had to be tested in the crucible of war—and at Tarawa it was.

As British Maj. Gen. John F. C. Fuller wrote in his history of the Second World War, amphibious warfare had been "revolutionized" at Tarawa by what was, "in all probability, the most far-reaching tactical innovation of the war."

Even by the time of the campaign against Kwajalein and others of the Marshall Islands, attack transports specially outfitted as communications centers became the command ships for amphibious assaults. *Maryland*'s transmitters, receivers, and associated antennae were too close together (and too close to the guns) and caused mutual interference. No other battleship would have been any better.

Navy underwater demolition teams now preceded the marines ashore and removed obstacles and mines in advance (and often left notes welcoming the marines ashore). This "innovation" had been recommended by Lt.

Col. Pete Ellis twenty years before, but his prescience had gone unrecognized until Tarawa. And after Tarawa, each Marine division had 300 amtracs to transport troops ashore plus another 25 to carry cargo.

An important contributor to the victory at Tarawa was the fact that the marines, their units originally in complete disarray, regrouped themselves into efficient fighting units of officers and men based solely on the groupings who found themselves sharing the same bit of beach at the same time.

Tarawa was a great lesson; it was also a great victory. The few Japanese prisoners from Tarawa told their interrogators that the thing that sent their morale plummeting from the first moment that the amtracs stopped on the reef was that the marines kept coming ashore in spite of machine-gun, artillery, and rifle fire even though many of them were wounded and their friends were dying all around them. The battle was finally won by Marine infantry. Without their ingenuity, skill, and, most of all, courage, nothing else would have mattered.

Receipt

No.   Date 6/9/16   19

Received From *Bernard Pierce*

Eighty Dollars   Dollars

For *OV*

Cash ☑   Check ☐

$ *80 00*

Due	$ 260	00
Paid	$ 80	00
Balance	$ 180	00

executive no. 7587

Appendix 1

Whatever Happened to . . . ?

Colonel David M. Shoup eventually became a four-star general and, in August 1959, was selected by President Eisenhower, over nine more senior generals, to become commandant of the Marine Corps. He later retired and lived quietly at his home in Arlington, Virginia, until his death at seventy-eight on January 13, 1983.

Colonel Merritt A. Edson retired as a major general in 1947, after serving on Saipan and Tinian. He died by his own hand in 1955 at age fifty-eight. The destroyer U.S.S. *Edson* was launched on January 5, 1958. Two of Edson's sons were serving as Marine officers at the time of his death.

Brigadier General Leo Hermle won a Navy Cross on Iwo Jima; he was commandant of the Marine Corps from 1946 to 1949. He retired from the Marine Corps in 1960 and died on January 21, 1976 as a lieutenant general.

Major General Julian Smith retired from the Marine Corps on December 1, 1946 as a lieutenant general; he died on November 5, 1975.

Major Henry Crowe won a Navy Cross at Tarawa and was wounded at Saipan. He went on to serve in Korea. After mandatory retirement at 62, he became the police chief of Portsmouth, Virginia.

Major Lawrence C. Hays served on Saipan, Tinian, and in Korea. He retired as a brigadier general on September 1, 1957.

Major William C. Chamberlin went on to the invasions of Saipan, Tinian, and Okinawa. He retired as a colonel with a Navy Cross in 1966.

Major Michael Ryan won a Navy Cross at Tarawa and went on to Saipan, Tinian, and Korea. He retired on July 1, 1977.

Lieutenant Colonel Kenneth F. McLeod was killed in action on Saipan.

Major Howard J. Rice was wounded at Saipan.

Major John F. Schoettel should have been court-martialed for his behavior at Tarawa, in the opinion of some of his colleagues. Shoup, however, did not agree. Schoettel was transferred to the Twenty-second Marines and was shore party commander on Eniwetok (where he was recommended for the bronze star). He was given command of another rifle battalion and was wounded on Guam but returned to duty. He was killed in action when the operation on Guam was nearly over.

Colonel Maurice Holmes retired as a brigadier general in 1946. He earned a PhD and has written a book on the Spanish exploration of California.

Major William K. Jones went on to the invasions of Saipan, Tinian, Okinawa, and to service in Vietnam. He became a lieutenant general and has since retired.

Lieutenant Colonel Raymond Murray was badly wounded on Saipan. He returned to serve in Korea and retired as a major general on August 1, 1968. He commanded the Fifth Marines in the breakout from the Chosin Reservoir during the Korean campaign.

Colonel Elmer Hall retired as a brigadier general in 1946; he died on September 23, 1958.

Brigadier General Thomas Bourke took part in the invasion of Saipan and would have commanded the Fifth Marine Division for the invasion of Japan. He died on January 5, 1978 at eighty-one.

Lieutenant Colonel Presley M. Rixey won a silver star on Tarawa and went on to take part in the actions on Tinian and Saipan. He retired as a brigadier general in 1957.

Lieutenant Colonel Alexander Swenceski spent nearly two years recovering from the severe injuries he received at Tarawa. He later served in Korea and retired as a brigadier general on May 31, 1955; he died on November 22, 1959.

APPENDIX 2

Marine Forces Involved in the Campaign for Tarawa Atoll

A reinforced Marine division consisted of five regiments, three of infantry (three battalions each), one artillery regiment (usually four battalions), and one engineer regiment (a shore party battalion, an engineer battalion, and a CB battalion), plus other elements such as a tank battalion. Each of the three infantry regiments had elements of artillery, engineers, etc., and thus reinforced became a regimental combat team. Each battalion landing team filled three attack transports and an attack cargo vessel (AKA).

Fifth Amphibious Corps
Commanding General: Maj. Gen. Holland M. Smith

    Second Marine Division
    Commanding General: Maj. Gen. Julian C. Smith
    Assistant Commander: Brig. Gen. Leo D. Hermle
    Chief of Staff: Col. Merritt A. Edson

      Second Marine Regiment (Second Marines):
        Commanding Officer: Col. David M. Shoup
        1st Battalion: Maj. Wood B. Kyle
        2nd Battalion: Lt. Col. Herbert R. Amey
        3rd Battalion: Maj. John F. Schoettel

Sixth Marine Regiment (Sixth Marines):
Commanding Officer: Col. Maurice G. Holmes
1st Battalion: Maj. William K. Jones
2nd Battalion: Lt. Col. Raymond L. Murray
3rd Battalion: Lt. Col. Kenneth F. McLeod

Eighth Marine Regiment (Eighth Marines):
Commanding Officer: Col. Elmer E. Hall
1st Battalion: Maj. Lawrence C. Hays, Jr.
2nd Battalion: Maj. Henry P. Crowe
3rd Battalion: Maj. Robert H. Ruud

Tenth Marine Regiment (Tenth Marines):
Commanding Officer: Brig. Gen. Thomas E. Bourke
1st Battalion: Lt. Col. Presley M. Rixey
2nd Battalion: Lt. Col. George R. E. Shell
3rd Battalion: Lt. Col. Manly L. Curry
4th Battalion: Lt. Col. Kenneth A. Jorgensen
5th Battalion: Maj. Howard V. Hiett

Eighteenth Marine Regiment (Eighteenth Marines):
Commanding Officer: Col. Cyril W. Martyr
1st Battalion: Maj. George L. H. Cooper
2nd Battalion: Lt. Col. Chester J. Salazar
3rd Battalion: Comdr. Lawrence E. Tull (U.S.N.)

2nd Amphibian Tractor Battalion:
Commanding Officer: Maj. Henry C. Drewes

2nd Tank Battalion:
Commanding Officer: Lt. Col. Alexander B. Swenceski

APPENDIX 3

Naval Forces Involved in the Campaign for Tarawa Atoll

Central Pacific Force (Task Group 51.1):
Vice Adm. Raymond A. Spruance (*Indianapolis*)
  Task Force 50, Carrier Force, Rear Adm. C. A. Pownell
    Carrier Interceptor Group: Carriers (CVs) *Yorktown* and *Lexington*, Light Carrier (CVL) *Cowpens*, Battleship (BB) *South Dakota*.
    Northern Carrier Group: Carrier *Enterprise*, Light Carriers *Belleau Wood* and *Monterey*, Battleships *Massachusetts, North Carolina*, and *Indiana*.
    Southern Carrier Group: Carriers *Essex* and *Bunker Hill*, Light Carrier *Independence*, Heavy Cruisers *Chester, Pensacola, Salt Lake City*, Light Cruiser *Oakland*.

  Task Force 57, Defense Forces and Shore-based Air, Rear Adm. J. H. Hoover

  Task Force 54, Assault Force, Rear Adm. R. K. Turner
    Headquarters Fifth Amphibious Corps, Maj. Gen. H. M. Smith, USMC
    Headquarters Support Aircraft, Col. W. O. Eareckson, USA
    Task Force 52, Northern Attack Force (Makin) Rear Adm. R. K. Turner

Task Force 53, Southern Attack Force (Tarawa) Rear Adm. H. W. Hill
Transport Group 4, Capt. H. B. Knowles, USN
   Attack Transports (APAs): *Zeilen, Heywood, Middleton, Biddle,
   Lee, Monrovia, Sheridan, LaSalle, Doyen, Harris, Bell,
   Ormsby,* and *Feland.*
   Attack Cargo Ships (AKAs): *Thuban, Virgo,* and *Bellatrix.*
   LSD: *Ashland* (joined at Efate).
Fire Support Group, Rear Adm. H. F. Kingman
   Battleships: *Tennessee, Maryland, Colorado.*
   Heavy Cruisers (CAs): *Portland, Indianapolis.*
   Light Cruisers (CLs): *Mobile, Birmingham, Santa Fe.*
   Destroyers (DDs): *Bailey, Frazer, Gansevoort, Meade, Anderson,
   Russell, Ringgold, Dashiell, Schroeder.*

Sources: An Annotated Bibliography

Anyone writing about an aspect of the Pacific war perforce begins with Admiral Samuel Eliot Morison's monumental study, *The United States Navy in World War II*. There are occasional errors in this massive work, but as most writers know, it is nearly impossible to produce one book entirely free of errors, let alone a dozen. A perfect book requires a perfect writer—and there aren't many of us left!

The "Holy Trinity" of books about the action on Tarawa Atoll itself begins with Robert Sherrod's book, *Tarawa: The Story of a Battle*, and continues with *Betio Beachhead* by Captain Wilson and his colleagues, and Captain Stockman's official account, *The Battle for Tarawa*. Sherrod's book was written while the sound, the stink, and the terror of the battle were still fresh in his mind; it is the record of a deeply felt personal experience, and in that context, it is unexcelled. But Sherrod's account is necessarily restricted to what he saw and heard during his time on Betio, and his mobility was naturally curtailed while the battle was in progress. The books of Wilson and his co-authors and of Stockman give a more detailed perspective of the battle in all its aspects than was available to Sherrod.

In what follows I have tried to indicate for most of the listed books those aspects I found particularly useful. I have read other books, or portions of books, in the preparation of this account, but they are not listed unless they contributed something that I did not already know. This is not a reflection on their quality but rather on the fact that I read them after I had already read other books that adequately covered the same material. The result is that some worthwhile books have been omitted from this list, which is restricted to those that actually contributed to this account.

And, of course, there are other books, in the seemingly infinite literature about various aspects of World War II, that I have not read at all. I make no apology for this. Life is short, and I wanted to get on with my own book after I felt that I had a reasonable understanding of the material I wanted to present.

Agawa, Hiroyuki. *The Reluctant Admiral: Yamamoto and the Imperial Navy.* Translated by John Bester. Tokyo: Kodansha International, 1979. Details of Yamamoto's personal and professional life and death.

Andrews, Captain Frank A. (USN, Ret.). *Torpedoes: Our Wonder Weapon (We Wonder if They'll Work).* Proceedings of the U.S. Naval Institute, March 1979.

Bailey, Ronald H. et al. *The Home Front.* Alexandria, VA: Time-Life Books, 1977. Rationing, etc.

Bailey, Tom. *Tarawa.* Derby, CN: Monarch Books, 1962.

Buell, Thomas B. *Master of Sea Power,* (E. J. King). Boston: Little, Brown, 1980. The Fleet Admiral's career, and King's problems with his colleagues and subordinates.

Cant, Gilbert. *The Great Pacific Victory.* New York: John Day, 1946. Naval strategy in the Pacific prior to Tarawa; good account of battle for Betio.

Craven, Wesley Frank, and Cate, James Lee. *The Army Air Forces in World War II,* Vol. 4. The Pacific: Guadalcanal to Saipan. Chicago: University of Chicago Press, 1958.

Crowl, Philip A., and Love, Edmund G. *The United States Army in World War II. The War in the Pacific. Seizure of the Gilberts and Marshalls, U.S. Army in World War II.* Washington, D.C.: Department of the Army, 1955. Good account of air actions of Army Air Forces in the Gilberts and postwar Japanese comments.

Donovan, Colonel James A. Jr. (USMC, Ret.). *The United States Marine Corps.* New York: Praeger, 1967.

Dull, Paul S. *A Battle History of the Imperial Japanese Navy (1941-45).* U.S. Naval Institute Press, 1978. Background of the Pacific war, Shinto, treaties, and conduct of the war from the Japanese point of view.

Dyer, Vice Admiral George C. (USN, Ret.). *The Amphibians Came to Conquer,* Vol. II. Washington, D.C.: U.S. Government Printing Office, 1969. Added detail to planning for Operation Galvanic, B-24 flights in detail, and battle itself.

Elson, Robert T. et al. *Prelude to War.* Alexandria, VA: Time-Life Books, 1976.

Farago, Ladislas. *The Broken Seal*. New York: Random House, 1967. U.S. and Japanese fleet problems and code breaking.

Forbis, William H. *Japan Today*. New York: Harper and Row, 1975.

Fuller, Major General John F. C. *The Second World War, 1939-45*. London: Eyre and Spottiswoode, 1948. Importance of amphibious techniques.

Grew, Joseph C. "Japan and the Pacific." *National Geographic*, April 1944. The Panay incident, etc.

Grimble, Sir Arthur. "War Finds its Way to the Gilbert Islands." *National Geographic*, January 1943.

Grosvenor, Melville Bell. "Landing Craft for Invasion." *National Geographic*, July 1944.

Hannah, Staff Sergeant Dick, USMC. *Tarawa*. Camera Publishing Corp., 1944.

Height, John McVicker, Jr. *FDR's "Big Stick."* Proceedings of The U.S. Naval Institute, July 1980.

Holmes, W. J. *Double-Edged Secrets*. Annapolis, MD: Institute Press, 1973. Details of Combined Fleet, work of the Combat Intelligence Unit, Rochefort.

Hoyt, Edwin P. *How They Won the War in the Pacific: Nimitz and His Admirals*. New York: Weybright and Talley, 1970. Good material including events surrounding Tarawa.

———. *Storm Over the Gilberts*. New York: Mason/Charter, 1978. Battle for Betio and the ordeal of *Independence*, Japanese response to invasion.

———. *Guadalcanal*. New York: Stein and Day, 1982.

Isely, Jeter A., and Crowl, Philip A. *The U.S. Marines and Amphibious War*. Princeton, NJ: Princeton University Press, 1951. As the title suggests this is an excellent account of the evolution of this important tactic. Also Gallipoli, and strategic and tactical aspects of the Pacific war prior to Tarawa.

Johnston, Richard W. *Follow Me. The Story of the Second Marine Division in World War II*. New York: Random House, 1948. Excellent book, good account of the division's stay in New Zealand.

Jones, Carl, USCG. "My First Day on Tarawa." In *The 100 Best True Stories of World War II*. New York: M. H. Wise, 1945.

Lifton, Robert J.; Kato, Suichi; and Reich, Michael R. *Six Lives, Six Deaths*. New Haven, CN: Yale University Press, 1979. Good source on Shinto, Japanese view of death.

Lord, Walter. *Incredible Victory*. New York: Harper and Row, 1967. Background material on Japan and the Battle of Midway.

McKiernan, Patrick L. *Tarawa: The Tide that Failed*. Proceedings of the U.S. Naval Institute, February 1962.

Manchester, William. *Good-bye Darkness*. Boston: Little, Brown, 1979. Personal account of life in the "old Corps" during World War II.

Martin, Ralph W. *The GI War*. Boston: Little, Brown, 1967. AKA loads and individual accounts of Tarawa.

Moore, Robert W. "Gilbert Islands in the Wake of Battle." *National Georgraphic*, February 1945.

Morison, Samuel Eliot. *History of United States Naval Operations in World War II*. Vol. I. *The Battle of the Atlantic*. Boston: Little, Brown, 1950. Naval history, treaties, Billy Mitchell, tactical developments.

―――. Vol. II. *Operations in North African Waters*. Early Higgins boats.

―――. Vol. III. *The Rising Sun in the Pacific*. Background of Pacific war in Japan and elsewhere, *Koda-Ha* etc., treaties, "incidents," Tripartite pact. SEM's view was that Yamamoto's strike on Pearl Harbor was a fatal mistake.

―――. Vol. IV. *Coral Sea, Midway, and Submarine Actions*. Early months of the Pacific war, approximately through Midway (June 1942).

―――. Vol. VI. *Breaking the Bismarcks Barrier*. Good background of Pacific war prior to Tarawa; JCS operations.

―――. Vol. VII. *Aleutians, Gilberts and Marshalls*. 1951. Pacific war just prior to and including Tarawa, tactical and strategic considerations, supply problems.

―――. *The Two-Ocean War*. Boston: Little, Brown, 1963. Decline of the U.S. Navy between the wars, Billy Mitchell, and much more (a condensation of his fourteen-volume account).

Pickins, Stuart D. B. *Shinto: Japan's Spiritual Roots*. Tokyo: Kodansha International, 1980. Mythology and Shinto.

Pierce, Lieutenant Colonel Philip N. (USMC, Ret.), and Hough, Lieutenant Colonel Frank O. *The Compact History of the United States Marine Corps*. New York: Hawthorne Books, 1964. Good account of the career of Pete Ellis.

Piggott, Juliet. *Japanese Mythology*. London: Paul Hamylin, 1969. Creation myths, Shinto, forty-seven *ronin*.

Pratt, Fletcher. *The Marines' War*. New York: William Sloane, 1948.

Reynolds, Clark G. *Famous American Admirals*. New York: Van Nostrand Reinhold, 1978.

―――. et al. *The Carrier War*, Alexandria, VA: Time-Life Books, 1982.

Rhoer, Edward Van der. *Deadly Magic*. New York: Scribner, 1978. Problems of changing codes, details of Yamamoto's schedule. Japanese strategic response to loss of Guadalcanal and Bougainville.

Richardson, W. *The Epic of Tarawa*. London: Odhams Press, 1945. Many errors.

Rosinski, Herbert. *The Development of Naval Thought*. Newport, RI: Naval War College Press, 1977. Good account of strategic position of

Japan as the war progressed and errors in the Japanese conception of the war.

Russ, Martin. *The Last Parallel.* New York: Rinehart and Co., 1957. Deals with the Korean War but good information on Marine weapons.

———. *Line of Departure.* New York: Doubleday, 1975.

Sakai, Saburo. *Samurai.* New York: Bantam, 1978. Air war from the viewpoint of Japan's most famous ace (64 confirmed kills).

Shapiro, Milton J. *Assault on Tarawa.* New York: McKay, 1981.

Shaw, Henry I. *Tarawa: A Legend Is Born.* New York: Ballantine, 1969.

Sherrod, Robert. *Tarawa: The Story of a Battle.* New York: Duell, Sloan, and Pierce, 1944, 1955, 1973. The basic account of the battle from Sherrod's viewpoint—unequaled since, but necessarily limited by Sherrod's restricted mobility under combat conditions.

Smith, Holland M., and Finch, Percy. *Coral and Brass.* New York: Scribner, 1949. The general's biography with his reasons for thinking Tarawa was a mistake and other background.

Steinberg, Rafael et al. *Island Fighting.* Alexandria, VA: Time-Life Books, 1978.

Stockman, Captain James R., USMC. *The Battle for Tarawa.* Historical Section, USMC, 1947. Everything about the battle itself.

Toland, John. *The Rising Sun.* New York: Random House, 1970. Excellent account of Japanese customs, folklore, and philosophy, and accurate translations of intercepted cables, Yamamoto's death.

Uris, Leon. *Battle Cry.* New York: Putnam, 1935. Not a very good novel but a source of useful information about the Marine Corps.

Vandegrift, General A. A., and Asprey, Robert C. *Once a Marine.* New York: Norton, 1964. Pete Ellis, New Zealand, Guadalcanal, Savo Island, etc.

The War Reports of General of the Army George Marshall, General of the Army H. H. Arnold, and Fleet Admiral Ernest King. New York: Lippincott, 1947. General strategic and tactical background; good account of the Battle of the Java Sea.

Wilson, Captain E. J., Lucas, Master Sergeant Jim G., Shaffer, Master Sergeant Samuel, and Zurlinden, Staff Sergeant C. Peter, USMC. *Betio Beachhead.* New York: Putnam, 1945.

Wyckoff, Colonel Don P. (USMC, Ret.). *Let There Be Built Great Ships. . . .* Proceedings of the U.S. Naval Institute, November 1982. Development of amtracs, Higgins boats, and LSTs.

Zich, Arthur et al. *The Rising Sun.* Alexandria, VA: Time-Life Books, 1977.

INDEX